*Great Houses of Italy*

# Great Houses of ITALY

*The Editors of Réalités*

*Preface by Jean Giono*

*G. P. Putnam's Sons New York*

This volume was conceived by
Gaston d'Angelis;
the text was under the direction of
Claude Frégnac;
Pierre Faucheux assisted by Michel Méline did
the layouts and typography.
Documentary illustrations were secured by
Claude Acremant;
the copy editor was Lambert Terbrack.

*We wish to express our most sincere thanks to the owners of the houses presented in this volume, who, by kindly providing us with the necessary documentation, enabled us to establish the historical texts and captions.*

*The realization of this work has been facilitated by:*
*His Excellency the French Ambassador to Rome*
*Doctor Luigi Mallé, Director of the City Museum of Turin*
*The Superintendant of Monuments of Piedmont*
*The Director General of the Secretariat of the Order of St. Maurice and St. Lazarus*
*The Superintendant of Museums for the provinces of Mantua, Verona and Cremona*
*The Director of the municipal library of Mantua*
*The Superintendant of Museums for the provinces of Florence, Arezzo and Pistoia*
*The Superintendant of Museums of the Marches*
*The Superintendant of Monuments of Latium*
*The Superintendant of Monuments of Campagnia*
*The Director of the Sicilian Ethnographic Museum*


First published in France in 1968 as *Merveilles des palais italiens*.

Published simultaneously in the Dominion of Canada by Longmans Canada Limited, Toronto.

Library of Congress Catalogue Card Number: 68-22256

PRINTED IN SWITZERLAND

# *Contents*

The first number refers to the page where the history of the house is recounted. The second number refers to the page where the illustrated description of the architectural features and the interior decor of the house begins.

# Picture credits

Pages

17. A regatta held September 21, 1775, in the gardens of the Villa Carpeneto.
17. Marie-Jeanne-Baptiste of Savoy-Nemours. Portrait. Seventeenth-century French school. Turin, Palazzo Madama.
18. The façade of the Palazzo Madama. Designed by Juvara. Turin, Museo Civico. Photo Rampazzi.
19. Palazzo Madama in 1649. Engraving by G. Tasnière. Turin, Museo Civico. Photo Rampazzi.
20. The Duchess Christina of France and her children. Seventeenth-century French school. Turin, Museo Civico. Photo Rampazzi.
20. Charles-Emmanuel I. Engraving by Petrus Rucholle after Van Dyck. Bibliothèque Nationale. Cabinet des Estampes. Photo Decordier.
21. Richard Wagner. Photo provided by the management of the Bayreuth Festival.
21. Josephine Grassini. Miniature on ivory by Ferdinand Quaglia. Bibliothèque Nationale. Photo Decordier.
22. Count Vitaliano Borromeo. Portrait by P. F. Cittadini. Villa Borromeo. Photo Desjardins.
22. Victor Amadeus II of Savoy.
23. Victor Emmanuel II in the uniform of the Grand Master of The Order of Saint Maurice. Stupinigi, Palazzina di Caccia.
30. Christina of France, Duchess of Savoy. Engraving by J. Frosne. Bibliothèque Nationale. Cabinet des Estampes. Photo Decordier.
45. Vue of the Palazzina di Caccia. Sketch by Juvara. Turin, Museo Civico. Photo Rampazzi.
51. Countess Isabella Teotochi-Albrizzi. Portrait by Madame Vigée-Lebrun, 1792. Gift of Edward Drummond Libby. Toledo, Museum of Art.
51. Charlotte Aglae d'Orleans. Portrait by Gobert. Versailles. French National Museums photo.
52. Marquis Benedetto Selvatico asking on behalf of Renaud d'Este, Duke of Modena, for the hand of the niece of the King of France for Francesco Maria d'Este. Painting. Palazzo Frigimelica-Selvatico. Photo A. Rubin/R. César.
52. Villa Valmarana. Engraving taken from Andrea Palladio's *I Quattro Libri dell' Architettura*. Bibliothèque Nationale. Photo Decordier.
53. Admiral Angelo Emo. Engraving. Bibliothèque Nationale. Cabinet des Estampes. Photo Decordier.
54. Admiral Angelo Emo. Portrait by Pietro Longhi. Venice, Palazzo Treves de' Bonfilii. Photo A. Rubin/R. César.
55. Giovanni Francesco Capodilista. Miniature taken from the manuscript of the Codice Capodilista. Bibliothèque de Padoue. Photo A. Rubin/R. César.
55. The Blessed Giordano Forzatè of Transalgardi, Bendictine abbot. Miniature taken from the manuscript of the Codice Capodilista. Bibliothèque de Padoue. Photo A. Rubin/R. César.
55. Pentesilea, Countess Capodilista. Padua, Museo Civico.
56. Marcantonio Barbaro. Portrait by Tintoretto. Vienna, Kunsthistorisches Museum.
57. Daniele Barbaro. Portrait by Paul Veronese. Florence, Pitti Palace. Photo A. Giraudon.
58. La Rotonda. Engraving from *I Quattro Libri dell' Architettura* by Andrea Palladio. Bibliothèque Nationale. Photo Decordier.
59. Andrea Palladio. Engraving by F. Zucchi, after Giovanni Battista Mariotti. Bibliothèque Nationale. Cabinet des Estampes. Photo Decordier.
97. Villa Barbaro at Maser. Engraving from *I Quattro Libri dell' Architettura* by Andrea Palladio. Bibliothèque Nationale. Photo Decordier.
103. The doge Leonardo Donà dalle Rose. Collection of Count Lorenzo Donà dalle Rose.
108. Villa Rotonda at Vicenza. Engraving from Andrea Palladio's *I Quattro Libri dell' Architettura* by Andrea Palladio. Bibliothèque Nationale. Photo Decordier.
111. Giuseppe Verdi. Engraving by Boldini. Private collection.
111. The Battle of Lepanto.
112. The Palazzo Durazzo-Pallavicini. Engraving. Bibliothèque Nationale. Cabinet des Estampes. Photo Decordier.

113. *Ariosto* by Titian. London, National Gallery. Photo Anderson-Giraudon.
114. *The Virgin of Victory* by Mantegna. Louvre Museum. Photo Giraudon.
115. *Pastoral Symphony* by Giorgione. Louvre Museum. Photo Giraudon.
116. Field Marshal Bettoni. Villa Bettoni. Photo A. Rubin/R. César.
117. Countess Francesca Gherardi. Portrait by Andrea Appiani. Photo A. Rubin/R. César.
118. Virgin and Child and members of the Maggi family. Villa Maggi. Photo A. Rubin/R. César.
119. Count Pietro Lechi. Pastel by Rosalba Carriera. Villa Lechi. Photo Nahmias.
124. View of the Palazzo Doria Principe. Engraving. Collection Doria Principe. Photo Renato Gasparini.
136. Portrait of Isabella d'Este. Drawing by Leonardo de Vinci. Louvre Museum. Photo Giraudon.
155. Marie-Madeleine. School of Rubens. Palazzo Corsini. Photo A. Rubin/R. César.
155. Cardinal Corsini. Portrait by Sustermans. Florence, Gallery Corsini.
156. Elisa Bonaparte, Princess Bacciochi. Bust by Chinard. Collection of the Count of Penha-Longa. Photo Giraudon.
156. Prince Felix Bacciochi. Bust by Chinard. Collection of the Count of Penha-Longa. Photo Giraudon.
157. Portrait presumed to be of Lucida Mansi. Photo A. Rubin/R. César.
158. The Boboli gardens at Florence. Engraving after Zocchi. Bibliothèque Nationale. Cabinet des Estampes. Photo Kalinine.
159. Francesco I de' Medici. Portrait by Bronzino. Florence, Pitti Palace. Photo Anderson-Giraudon.
159. Luca Pitti. Fifteenth-century fired clay. Florence, Pitti Palace. Photo Alinari-Giraudon.
160. Bianca Cappello. Portrait by Alessandro Allori. Florence, Pitti Palace. Photo Anderson-Giraudon.
161. Baldassar Castiglione. Portrait by Raphael. Louvre Museum. Photo Bulloz.
162. Battista Sforza, Duchess of Urbino. Portrait by Piero della Francesca. Florence, Uffizi Museum. Photo Anderson-Giraudon.
162. Federigo Montefeltro, Duke of Urbino. Portrait by Piero della Francesca. Florence, Uffizi Museum. Photo Anderson-Giraudon.
163. *The Venus of Urbino* by Titian. Florence, Uffizi Museum. Photo Giraudon.
165. Palazzo Corsini, Florence. Engraving. Bibliothèque Nationale. Cabinet des Estampes. Photo Decordier.
175. Villa Reale at Marlia. Engraving from *Passegiata in Villa.* Photo Office of Tourism, Rome.
185. Pitti Palace in Florence. Engraving. Bibliothèque Nationale. Cabinet des Estampes. Photo Decordier.
193. Allegory of the Triumph of Battista Sforza, Duchess of Urbino, by Piero della Francesca. Florence, Uffizi Museum. Photo Anderson-Giraudon.
199. Andrea Doria. Portrait by Sebastiano del Piombo. Rome, Palazzo Doria Pamphili. Photo Alinari-Giraudon.
199. Giannettino Doria. Portrait by Bronzino. Rome, Palazzo Doria Pamphili. Photo Alinari-Giraudon.
201. The "Stanza di Apollo" at Frascati. Engraving by Giovanni Battista Falda. Villa Aldobrandini. Photo Desjardins.
202. Elisabeth Farnese. Portrait by Van Loo. Versailles. Photo Archives photographiques.
204. Cardinal Scipion Borghese. Bust by Bernini. Rome, Borghese Gallery. Photo Alinari-Giraudon.
205. Fountain "della Civetta" in the Tivoli gardens. Engraving by Giovanni Francesco Venturini. Bibliothèque Nationale. Cabinet des Estampes. Photo Decordier.
206. Franz Liszt around 1882. Photo Louis Held/Weimar.
207. Plan of the Villa Farnese at Caprarola. Bibliothèque Nationale. Cabinet des Estampes. Photo Decordier.
223. View of the gallery of the villa Farnese. Hand-colored engraving done in 1777 after a design by Francesco Panini and Lodovico Tesco. Villa Farnese. Photo Nahmias.
234. Villa Lante at Bagnaia. Engraving. Bibliothèque Nationale. Cabinet des Estampes. Photo Decordier.
255. Lucrezia Borgia. Fresco by Pinturicchio in the Borgia apartments. The Vatican Palace. Photo Anderson-Giraudon.
256. Alphonso I d'Este, Duke of Ferrara. Portrait by Dosso Dossi. Modena, Estense Gallery. Photo Alinari-Giraudon.
256. Ercole I d'Este, Duke of Ferrara. Portrait by Dosso Dossi. Modena, Estense Gallery. Photo Anderson-Giraudon.
257. Niccolò II d'Este. Manuscript N° 293. Rome, National Library. Photo Dr. M. Vivarelli and V. Gulla.
258. Prince Giampaolo Maria de Soragna. Seventeenth-century Italian school. Photo A. Rubin/R. César.
258. Ottavia Rossi di San Secondi, Princess of Soragna. Seventeenth-century Italian school. Photo A. Rubin/R. César.
259. Permit giving the count of Soragna the right to return to Parma. La Rocca di Soragna. Photo A. Rubin/R. César.
279. Queen Caroline Murat and her children. Portrait by Gérard. Musée de Malmaison. Collection of His Highness Prince Charles Murat. Photo Giraudon.
281. Admiral Nelson. Portrait by L.F. Abbott. London, National Portrait Gallery.
281. Lady Hamilton. Portrait by Romney. Cranbury Park Collection. Document provided by the Medici Society Ltd., London.
283. Murat, King of Naples. Portrait by Gérard. Collection of His Highness Prince Murat. Photo Bulloz.

Isola Bella
Villa Borromeo
LOMBARDY
VENETIA
Maser
Villa Barbaro
Bogliaco
Villa Bettoni
Calino
Villa Maggi
Milan
Villa Rotonda
Villa Valmarana dei Nani
Vicenza
Villa Pisani
Verona
Stra
PIEDMONT
Venice
Palazzo Donà dalle Rose
Palazzo Albrizzi
Palazzo Treves de' Bonfilii
Padua
Palazzo Emo Capodilista
Palazzo Frigimelica-Selvatico
Villa Lechi
Palazzina di Caccia
Stupinigi
Turin
Royal Palace
Palazzo Madama
Villa Carpeneto
Mantua
Reggia
Palazzo del Tè
Parma
Rocca di Soragna
Ferrara
Castello Estense
EMILIA-ROMAGNA
Genoa
Palazzo Doria Principe
Palazzo Pallavicini
Palazzo Durazzo-Pallavicini
LIGURIA
Bologna
Palazzo Montanari
Ravenna
Villa Reale
Marlia
Pitti Palace
Palazzo Corsini
Segromigno Monte
Villa Mansi
Florence
Giogoli
Villa dei Collazzi
Urbino
Ducal Palace
MARCHES
TUSCANY
Perugia
Bagnaia
Villa Lante
Caprarola
Villa Farnese
Palazzo Farnese
Palazzo Doria Pamphili
Palazzo Rospigliosi-Pallavicini
Tivoli
Villa d'Este
Rome
Frascati
Villa Aldobrandini
LATIUM
Caserta
Royal Palace
Naples
CAMPANIA
Bari
Sassari
Cagliari
Messina
Palermo
La Favorita
Palazzo Gangi
Bagheria
Villa Palagonia
SICILY
Catania

# *Preface*

*Architecture is not an entity in itself. It must harmonize with a particular sky, a light, or some virtue of its geographical setting, especially that Italian* virtù *which is a voluptuousness of the soul.*

*The Via Garibaldi of Genoa, originally Strada Maggiore, then Strada Aurea, which Mme. de Staël called the "Street of Kings," was opened in 1550 with no thought of glory but merely to improve a quarter consisting of huts and alleys. Place it in Edinburgh—one of the finest cities in the North—and it will be nothing more than Princes Street. Here it becomes iridescent. Yet the final designs of Cantone de Cobio, Galeazzo Alessi, Rocco Lurago, Giovan Battista Castello and Filippo Parodi would not have succeeded in giving it its flash of color if, at first, they had not harmonized with this sea and no other, this sky and these steep slopes, these winds from Piedmont and glimmers from distant Lombardy. What would Bologna be if her architects had not considered the sparkling Emilian poplars? Ravenna if they had not been governed by the dunes? And Venice if they had not been attentive to the lapping lagoons and the Adriatic storms? Rome was Rome before the Romans, with her red marshes, her vermilion oaks, her dry horizons; but the builders' virtue lay in knowing that they could not erect just anything in this arena and that, before using a plumb line, they had to listen, see and feel.*

*A roof is worth only what the heart is worth. Beauty was once the principal requirement; the peristyle was built before the sanitary block, for the hygiene of the soul.*

*Some small valley of the Tuscan Apennines suggested the rather unnatural villa, barren nine feet above the ground, the windows narrow and covered with bramble, all, with the exception of the last ones, open to the slopes downvalley. Level with the roof they could be enlarged into galleries where one could observe the countryside. If it is said today that in a century of missiles why not after all build a "glass house" here, one realizes that such a house would fail to fulfill its role. One evening a bronze twilight colored with blood in the heights penetrates too strongly through the large bay windows; one day the foxes howl too loudly, there is too much noise from the wind and rumbling in the distance; one morning the light is too bright, one afternoon the rain brings too many smells or there is too much sunshine—in short, there is a general discord with the timeless established order without which, before anything else, one cannot live in peace.*

*Italy has always been very clever in understanding this "before anything else." For all man's orbiting into space, there remains the earth on which he is obliged to keep his feet. The days consist of thousands of living moments with which one must constantly be in harmony. The Mediterraneans (Phoenicians, Greeks, Cretans and others) had deified these moments. Then a rumor spread that Pan was dead, but it was untrue and well-informed people soon knew this.*

*Mathematics is fine, yet east of the site where I am going to build stands an ilex wood. These oaks with their strong leaves reflect the heat like a mirror, and I must take this into consideration. Every morning at the height of summer as the sun rises there comes a torrid gust from that direction. Two and two equal four, but before me are the melancholy poplars, and this is fine if I like melancholy. If I am afraid, two and two will henceforth merely equal three, and certainly the solution will not be to cut down these poplars, for that would be too simple. The gods are never simple.*

*This is the substance of Italian grace. It never depends upon the simplicity of the gods; it knows that mathematics is nothing more than the refuge of those who lack love. Italian grace has the necessary intelligence of knowing what comes before anything else.*

*Piedmont in its semicircle of Alps topped by Mont Blanc, with its clumps of poplars, its foaming torrents, steep slopes and vermilion hills, its vineyards and its small roads bordered by reeds, rises in great severe flanks, with large vestibules and winding slopes which from section to section shoot up toward the open skies paned with gray. All that is lacking in the vineyards of Asti, the nocturnal groanings of the alders of Alexandria, the lofty hills of Savona, Piedmont puts into the architecture of its palaces, its castles, its villas and the arrangement of its gardens. There is no possibility of a mistake: nothing that has been built here can be transplanted without damage or peril; the complement would no longer harmonize and the heart's reckoning no longer be exact.*

*The same is true of Bologna, Mantua, Florence, Pisa, Rome, Naples, and even the small towns lost in the cloudy valleys, where the dusty roads are swept solely by the wind, and the villages that are effaced by their mimesis of stone. Palaces, castles, villas and gardens were not designed and then built for the sake of praise but for selfish and often solitary enjoyment.*

*If this pond with its crying fountains has bedded itself into the walls as though covered with myrtle, it was to enable the sound of these amplified cries, embellished by sonorous shadows and echoes, to affect nostalgically these curtain walls at the far end of the north chamber. No doubt there was once a lady here, or a soldier, even a bishop or a cardinal fond of a melancholy dream to which corresponded a massive main building, a labyrinth of box trees, landings and steps used by hired assassins.*

*A few miles from Rome a path skirts the low hills in the midst of a forest of small oaks. The only sound is that of the grasshopper. The sky is plaster gray. In this pale dryness stands a "pleasure" villa, and everything combines to make this desert a place of pleasure. From the travertine walls, whose reddish brown harmonizes with the funerary gray, softens it and gives it its quality of paradise, right down to the windows with their small panes outlined with lead, everything is built to function within this dust and torrid air, this permanent assault of heat and glaring light. The interior is the color of autumn fruit in whose juice one already catches a glimpse of winter. It is not the color of the plaster on the walls but the interlacing of contrasting rays through the panes that produces a gleam of vermilion (which never breaks up the shadow but illuminates it) to reassure and amuse the eye. The color is chosen not by the painter but by the architect who has judiciously combined both the surface of these openings and their orientation. In this gleam, the staircases rise like shavegrass, the corridors plunge ahead like brushwood, the rough coat of plaster scintillates like some forest depth; a well-being of imagination relieves one of the harshness of the outer deserts.*

*Around Brescia, Verona and the lakes, along the Mincio River, in the reeds of the Mantuan swamps, in the midst of the Virgilian vineyards and the trees of the Vicenzan orchards, among the alders and aspens of the Po, slumber the huge houses and great gardens that a way of life—"the art of living"—first inspired in the human heart. Long before the architect had summoned the workmen, even before the first drawings, the villa, the castle, the palace, the lawns, the labyrinth, the copse, the card-designed verdure, the rose gardens, the multicolored checkered pattern, the shrubbery of the composed landscape—all existed in the minds of those who sought to possess these important aids to happiness. The idea had long been a cherished dream, even when it was that of a powerful lord or banker, who merely had to say the word for his dream to become a reality. The word was not said at once: "before anything else" required counsel of the country, the seasons, the skies, the compass dial; and it was only after everything else had been properly taken into account that the architect, the mason, even the workmen were chosen, then the stone and its sculptors, the wood and its carpenters, the clay and its ceramists, the plaster and its plasterers, the lime and its fresco artists, confronting the architecture every moment to draw it up to its full height with a world already in place so that there would be perfect harmony between them.*

*These houses have a soul and are physical beings. One merely has to glance, for example, at the Palazzina di Caccia at Stupinigi, near Turin. Here is the personality of a Baroque courtier. The dignity of ducal hunts, festivities, balls and the wonders of royal diversions are his domain. A* palazzina *speaks of a flight of hawks heading for the clouds, of a boar at bay, of hunters loaded with their catch.*

*Msgr. Paolo Almerico, referendary of Pius IV and Pius V, commissioned Palladio to design a villa at Vicenza which would be a refuge for his old age when the problems of precedence would have ceased to exist. "Build me 'democratic' rooms," he said to the architect, and as he pronounced this word he made a circular gesture. The villa became the Rotonda.*

*These palaces and gardens were above all games, like chess, checkers, spillikins and cards, before becoming shelters, retreats, fortresses or even proud possessions.*

*The condottiere who temporarily left camp and his men wanted to enjoy his house. It had to preserve a martial atmosphere yet not be without tenderness. The pleasant moments of the day, which the soldier would not enjoy in his tent, were expected at home, with these corridors,* trompe-l'oeil *frescoes and huge salons which echoed his steps. He arranged the shadows to his height and the echoes whose sound his soul interpreted with the chief Italian joy of analyzing the very moment. What for others was but a second was for him an infinite series of occasions for sensations.*

*Such were the games of the condottiere and the cardinal, the patrician and the wealthy merchant, the banker, duke, prince and king. For some it was a question of reflections in the shade, for others corridors, staircases, ballrooms, vestibules, terraces, towers, balconies, belvederes, underground communications, secret doors, concealed passages, forests, columns, plastering, frescoes, statues, fine wood.*

*The brocaded robes of some needed gleaming stone floors, while the cardinalate robes of another required plane- or lemon-tree panelling. A man who burned charcoal in the brazier of his bank would want a fireplace capable of consuming an oak, while another who was usually galloping at the head of his lancers in some desolate open countryside enjoyed the luxury of large windows "thirty feet high," facing weeping willows, thick grass and sparkling fountains. This little man wearing a velvet* biretta, *his fingers worn from holding a buckler, would ask for rather generous allegories of Venuses (disguised as madonnas) and fleshy nymphs, narrow rooms, alcoves, historiated walls in imitation of forest depths. And this tall dry fellow whose bone joints crackle louder than the joints of his armor would need large staircases with small flat steps, deep windows framed by stone benches, huge spaces, high ceilings, immense rooms where he could indulge his slight limp with impunity, and corners enclosed by screens where, curled up like a dog, he could warm his pains, as was the case in the Palazzo Cangrande at Verona.*

*It was not so much comfort that was wanted as pleasure. Although the house was beautiful only on the exterior, it was the inmates who benefitted. Here the exteriors were conceived merely as costumes, which they are, but the interiors were habitable souls, thanks to architecture and its associated professions. Instead of going to a philosopher for a new soul, one built an enclosure whose proportions, temporarily at first, gave one the desired soul.*

*Thus the behavior of the Medici is explained by so many feet of façade and tons of diamond-shaped stone; the Este and Gonzaga remain jealous of one another's palaces; the Borromeo family rather haughtily bristle their balustrades with nymphs, goddesses and Roman rulers; the Farnese of Capraro naively reveal the darkness in their hearts, the Orsini of Bomarzo are worried, the Este of Cennobbio and the Crivelli of Inverizo are reassured and the Bombici of Florence fascinated.*



*Villa Marcello at Levade*

*Every palace, castle and villa is a victory snatched from the human condition. Thus from Genoa to Naples, from Turin to Venice, from Bologna to Rome, from Ravenna to Grossetto, passions are crystallized: here on the edge of a path, there on the crest of a hill, elsewhere in the plains, often on the banks of rivers, in former times in solitude and deserts. This man was arrogant, that one boastful, here is the heroic one, there the amorous one. Some have immortalized their bravery, others their jealousy. Like those blonde shells which growing grasshoppers leave stuck to blades of grass or to the rough bark and which down to the slightest detail reproduce the form of the insect, these castles, palaces and villas emerging from the silhouette of Italy enable us today to understand down to the most trifling peculiarity the passions of the masters who built them.*

*Jean Giono,* Académie Goncourt

According to Charles de Brosses, the great eighteenth-century French scholar who devoted a lifetime to studying the Italian land and people, the ambition of every Italian lord was "to leave his name, his magnificence and his taste to posterity." It is to this concern for glory that we are indebted for the Italian palazzos with majestic or restrained façades bordering the city streets, and the villas scattered throughout the countryside, stone mingling with trees and fountains to recreate the landscape and, in a way, to frame it in scenery conceived with strict harmony. A century later Hippolyte Taine wrote that the dream of everyone who owned a palazzo was for it "to become a museum whose name would be listed in guidebooks." Consequently the greatest painters were summoned to decorate the walls and ceilings, and works of art furnished the apartments. In retracing the history of the families who erected the most magnificent houses of the peninsula, in recalling the names of the condottieri, prelates and princes enamored of glory and art, the whole history of Italy comes to life again with all its *éclat*.

# *Piedmont*

*Hemmed in by the Western Alps and the first ridges of the Apennines lies Piedmont or "country at the base of mountains." From the French border to Lake Maggiore and Lake Ticino, its meadows and its wheat and rice fields are spread out over both banks of the Po River. Long lines of poplars break up this rich plain crossed by the Po and its tributaries, flanked on the south by the Montferrat Hills. To the east and to the north are the Alpine passes and valleys, whose possession made the counts of Savoy, the masters of Piedmont in the eleventh century, the gate keepers of the Alps. Taking clever advantage of their situation bordering on France, Switzerland and Germany, becoming at times the allies of the Hapsburgs, at others of the Bourbons, they continued to increase their domains. Finally in 1713 their royal dignity was recognized at the Treaty of Utrecht, but Savoy was obliged to exchange Sicily for Sardinia in 1720. The rise of the house of Savoy resumed in 1859. It acquired the crown of Italy in 1861 and retained it until 1946.*

## Turin *Villa Carpeneto*

The domain of Carpeneto was acquired on February 17, 1643, from Countess Girolama Valperga by Gaspare Graneri, who was president and general of finance at the court of Turin. One of his sons, Marcantonio, was first chaplain to the Duke of Savoy. Another, named Tomaso, acquired the marquisate in 1682 and succeeded his father as president of finance of Savoy in 1687.

The domain was originally a fortress which as early as the middle of the seventeenth century was converted into a villa. The present edifice, however, was reconstructed in 1769-1770 by the Marquis Luigi Maria Graneri della Rocca, ambassador at Moscow, from the design by the architect Francesco Valeriano dellala di Beinasco. King Charles Albert stayed in the villa on several occasions and it was here that he wrote his booklet *My Evenings at Carpeneto.*

The Graneri family died out at the close of the nineteenth century and the

*Fête in the Carpeneto gardens*

domain was sold. It was owned by various persons until acquired by Count Theo Rossi di Montelera, who restored the villa to its original splendor.

## Turin *Palazzo Madama*

In 1632, Christina of France, Duchess of Savoy, daughter of Henri IV and wife of Victor Amadeus I, together with members of the court, assisted from the balcony of the Palazzo Madama at a splendid fête given on the occasion of the birth of the princely heir, François-Hyacinthe. The event had been greeted with particular enthusiasm, since the duke and duchess had until then nothing but daughters. (The child, however, lived only a few months after the death of his father in 1637, and he was succeeded in 1638 by his younger brother, Charles Emmanuel, born in 1634.)

The theme of the fête was "the Triumph of Joy in the World": allegorical chariots representing the Virtues and Triumphs promised to the newborn child (on one of them could be seen the cradle of Jupiter). But the chief attraction of the ceremony was the combat between four cavalry squadrons commanded by the Duke of Savoy, Don Maurice, Don Felix of Savoy (the natural son of the Duke Emmanuel Philibert), and Marshal Toiras on the one hand and, on the other, a centaur, a hydra, a lion and a dragon—cardboard monsters symbolizing Savagery, Idleness, Anger and Dishonor. Among the spectators was Mazarin, then at the beginning of his career, who, after the Casal Affair, acted as intermediary between Louis XIII and the Duke of Savoy.

The Palazzo Madama was built on the site of the Roman Porta Decumana which was subsequently englobed in the construction dating from different periods. As early as the tenth and eleventh centuries, the Roman monuments were rebuilt and additions made. From 1276 to 1280 Guglielmo VII, Marquis of Montferrat, added a fortress which in 1280 he was obliged to cede to Thomas III (1252-1282), Count of Piedmont, founder of the branch of Achaïe of the House of Savoy. The wedding of Galeazzo II Visconti, Lord of Milan, and Blanche of Savoy was celebrated here on September 28, 1350. At the beginning of the fifteenth century, Ludovic d'Achaïe replaced the thirteenth-century constructions with a more important fortress, also built on to the Roman gate and enclosed by a square courtyard. The building still forms the nucleus of the present-day edifice and the façade, facing the Po, although very much remodelled, dates from this period. Work was scarcely finished when Ludovic d'Achaïe, several months before his death in 1418, here received Pope Martin V, who was returning from the Council of Constance. That same year the Achaïe branch died out with Ludovic, and Piedmont and Turin were inherited by Amadeus VIII (1383-1451), first Duke of Savoy and future Pope Felix V.

Charles VIII, while en route to Italy to conquer the Kingdom of Naples, stayed in the palace in 1495. In 1535 Turin and Piedmont were occupied by French troops and Emmanuel Philibert (1528-1580) who, two years after winning the Battle of Saint-Quentin in 1557, married Marguerite, the daughter of Francis I, did not regain his states until 1562.

The duke and his court did not then reside at the Palazzo Madama but at the bishop's palace, situated approximately at the site of a wing of the present royal palace; the two edifices were connected by a gallery erected in 1497 which Charles Emmanuel I (1562-1630) magnificently decorated and where he installed his collection of paintings and works of art. However, the Palazzo Madama was often used for courtly fêtes, especially theatrical spectacles. It was here in 1585, on the occasion of the wedding of Charles Emmanuel I and Catherine of Hapsburg, daughter of Philip II, that one of the first performances, probably partial, was given of the "Pastor Fido" by Giovanni Battista Guarini; the work was not published until 1590 and the official "première" took place at Crema in 1595.

The edifice, however, must have appeared quite old-fashioned and in 1608 the façade facing the Piazza Castello was redecorated for the marriage of the daughters of Charles Emmanuel, Francesco of Mantua and Alfonso of Modena. The fêtes given in the palace were splendid: the dinner "by small tables" and "in the Chinese fashion" was considered a particularly original innovation. In 1619 the façade facing the square was again modified in the classic style.

*Marie-Jeanne-Baptiste of Savoy-Nemours*

The great period of the Palazzo Madama began in 1637 when the widow of Victor Amadeus I, Christina of France, "Madama Reale" (after whom the palace was named), ruled in the name of her young sons, François-Hyacinthe, who died in 1638, then the latter's brother, Charles Emmanuel II. Intelligent and energetic, supported by her favorite, Count Philippe d'Aglie, the regent played a difficult role, caught between her brothers-in-law, the Cardinal Maurice of Savoy and Prince Thomas de Carignan, both devoted to Spain and France, who enjoyed their preference but whose designs on Savoy rightly worried her. Christina soon found herself in open warfare against her brothers-in-law. She sought refuge at Chambéry where she had a stormy meeting with Louis XIII and Richelieu, refusing to leave her son as hostage and ceding her fortresses. The French besieged Turin and after many difficulties conquered the Spanish forces and those of the Prince de Carignan; but the regent made her entry into the city dressed in mourning to show her dissatisfaction. Finally in

*Façade of the Palazzo Madama*

June, 1642, Christina was reconciled with Carignan and the cardinal who, forsaking the Church, married her thirteen-year-old niece, Louisa Christina.

On becoming regent, Christina had decided to abandon the bishop's palace for the Palazzo Madama, which was easier to defend and where she felt safer. But raised in the luxury of the French court, she wanted to make it a real royal residence. Important work was undertaken as early as 1638 and in spite of interruptions during the siege of Turin, the construction was soon finished in 1642. The inner courtyard of the old fifteenth-century castle was replaced, on the first floor, by a huge salon supported by vaults occupying the ground floor. Magnificent suites were decorated for the regent, the young duke and their attendants. The decoration work was finished about 1649; at that date a new façade adorned with classic orders was erected on the Piazza Castello.

Madama Reale died in 1663. Her end was edifying: she made frequent retreats at the Carmelites of Turin, wore a hair shirt, had herself scourged, assisted on her knees at fifteen successive masses and, spread out at the chapel door, insisted that the nuns, after the service, place their heels on her throat, as though she were being trampled.

Charles Emmanuel II had in 1663 married Françoise d'Orléans, his first cousin, daughter of his mother's brother, Gaston d'Orléans. The following year, however, his wife died and he shut himself up in the Palazzo Madama during the ensuing months. In 1665 he was married again to Marie-Jeanne-Baptiste of Savoy-Nemours and then in 1675 disappeared to history's view. Marie-Jeanne-Baptiste took the title of regent for her son Victor Amadeus II (1666-1732) and settled at the Palazzo Madama.

Madly in love with power, the second Madama Reale thought for a time of marrying her son to her niece, Isabella, daughter of her sister, Maria Louisa, wife of Alfonso II, then of Peter II of Portugal, heir to the throne of Braganza: Victor Emmanuel would have thus abandoned to his mother his Savoyard states, whose regency she would have retained. The young king refused this proposition and in 1686, after a palace revolution, he freed himself from his mother's yoke and governed alone. Madama consoled herself with difficulty. Henceforth her authority extended only over questions of etiquette—she was very fussy about such matters—and in the palace she undertook numerous and costly works.

She partly remodelled and completed the decoration of her suites, whose splendor equalled that of her son's royal palace. The inventory made after her death mentions the prodigious quantity of sumptuous fabrics and porcelain and above all of furniture and silver objects accumulated there. Access to the salons on the first floor, however, was always by means of a small obscure flight of steps situated in the tower. Madama Reale wanted an entrance and staircase worthy of her residence and in 1718 she commissioned Filippo Juvara to design the superb façade and the staircase of honor, finished in 1721, which are today the finest parts of the palace.

On the death of Jeanne-Marie-Baptiste in 1724, the palace was only intermittently occupied: the future Charles Emmanuel IV and his wife, Madame Clotilde, sister of Louis XVI, resided here at the close of the eighteenth century. During the French occupation it became the seat of the provisional government in 1799. It was scheduled to be demolished, but in 1800 only a part of the gallery which connected it with the royal palace was destroyed. In 1805 General Menou, administrator general of Piedmont, wanted to raze it again. Taking advantage of the Emperor's passing through Turin, he tried to obtain authorization to destroy what he called "this old shanty." Napoleon went to the palace and, marvelling at Juvara's work, tapped Menou on the shoulder and said ironically, "It's you, my good Menou, who are an old shanty!" The palace was then used to house the Court of Appeal. In 1814 it was invaded by the populace who threw from the windows all the dossiers accumulated by the French administration.

In 1832 Charles Albert hung most of the paintings of the royal collections in the suites open to the public; this is now the Galleria Sabauda. Beginning in 1848 the Subalpine Senate met in the large salon arranged for this purpose until it was transferred to Florence in 1865. It was here that Victor Emmanuel II swore to uphold the Constitution of 1849 after the abdication of Charles Albert. In the same salon on April 2, 1860, after the annexation of Tuscany, Emilia and Romagna, the king inaugurated the first parliament of northern and central Italy and made a speech which roused the enthusiasm of the Chamber, stating that in a few years Lombardy "had been freed, thanks to the great achievements of the armies" and central Italy "thanks to the splendid virtue of the people." The following year, after the annexation of the Kingdom of Naples, of the Marches and of Umbria, this assembly became the first Italian parliament.

*Palazzo Madama in the seventeenth century*

After the transfer of the government to Florence, the palace served as the seat of the Supreme Court of Appeal until 1925. It was restored on several occasions. Since 1927 it has been used by the Turin municipality for official celebrations and since 1933 it has contained the Museo Civico di Arte Antica with its superb collection of paintings, sculptures and decorative arts.

## Turin *Royal Palace*

On March 23, 1848, King Charles Albert solemnly left the throne room of the Palace and from the balcony of the adjacent weapons gallery made the famous speech which marked the beginning of the Italian War of Independence. At the beginning of the year Lombardy and Venetia had rebelled against Austrian domination, and the king, swayed by liberal Piedmont and Sardinian opinion (on March 4 he had granted his people a constitution, the *Statuto*), decided to declare war against Austria and to support the insurgents, bringing them "the aid that one brother expects from another." It was also during the same speech, refusing the aid that Minister of foreign affairs Alphonse Lamartine and the French provisional government had offered, that Charles Albert launched the famous statement, *"L'Italia fara da se"* (Italy will do so alone), a statement which events were cruelly to belie. Marshall Radetzky, at the head of the Austrian troops, inflicted a crushing defeat on the Piedmont troops at Custozza on July 24-25, 1848, then at Novara on March 23, 1849, exactly a year after the proclamation. Charles Albert abdicated that same evening and withdrew to a Portuguese convent, where he died four months later. For his son, Victor Emmanuel II, was reserved the task of uniting Italy with the aid of Napoleon III.

The present royal palace has replaced more ancient edifices, the residence of the dukes of Savoy since the fifteenth century. One of these, the bishop's palace, dated from the medieval period. Emmanuel Philibert (1528-1580) had erected alongside a building known as the palace of Saint John which was subsequently enlarged for Charles Emmanuel I (1562-1630).

In 1645, the widow of Victor Amadeus I (1587-1637), Christina of France, ruling for her son Charles Emmanuel II (1634-1675), decided to raze all these buildings and replace them with a more impressive palace. Amedeo di Castellamonte designed the façade, which was erected in 1658-1659. Work continued rather slowly, but the central building and a section of the east wing were finished by 1663 when Charles Emmanuel II married Françoise d'Orléans, his cousin and daughter of Gaston d'Orléans. It is Charles Emmanuel to whom we are indebted for the Chapel of the Holy Shroud erected by Guarino Guarini.

Construction of the palace continued during the following reigns. In 1720 Filippo Juvara built the staircase known as "delle Forbici" (of the scissors) which connected the first and second floors. Meanwhile a whole team of painters sumptuously decorated the suites, especially the handsome large gallery.

A rather clever sovereign, skillfully weighing himself between France, Spain and Austria, Victor Amadeus obtained the crown of Sicily at the

Treaty of Utrecht in 1713, but after the Treaty of London in 1718 he was obliged to exchange Sicily for Sardinia. Such greatness raised the House of Savoy to the heights of the leading ruling families of Europe. Victor Amadeus' ties with the House of France were numerous; in 1684 he had married Anne-Marie d'Orléans, daughter of Monsieur, Louis XIV's brother, and of Henrietta of England; and their daughter was to become the charming Duchess of Burgogne.

Was it the example of Louis XIV that inspired Victor Amadeus to establish at the court of Turin the reign of

*Christina of France and her children*

"declared mistresses"? His long liaison with the Countess of Verrue is one of the most amorous romantic adventures. Born in 1670, the daughter of a second marriage of the Duke of Luynes and Anne de Rohan, Mme. de Verrue was married at the age of thirteen and a half to Marie-Joseph-Ignace de Scaglia, Count of Verrue, whose mother, originally French, was lady of honor to the dowager duchess of Savoy. The young couple left for Turin well satisfied with their lot. "The Count de Verrue," stated Saint-Simon, "was handsome, well built, rich, witty and a fine gentleman. She also was witty and her mind was turned in the direction of government. They were much in love with each other and spent several happy years. . ." However short this period of happiness, Mme. de Verrue presented her husband with three children.

The young wife was quite beautiful and attracted the attention of Victor Amadeus. "She observed this," related Saint-Simon, "and told her husband and mother-in-law, who were content to praise her and asked no questions." The duke insisted. Mme. de Verrue tried to escape his close attention and asked permission not to appear at court any longer but "the old lady (her mother-in-law) became angry, quarelled with her, told her that she wanted to give herself airs and that her imagination was aroused by her vanity." The husband sided with his mother. Exasperated, the young woman pretended to be ill and received permission, escorted by her husband's uncle, the abbot of Verrue, to go to Bourbon, a spa in France, where she begged her father to join her. Frightened by his daughter's story, the Duke de Luynes wanted her to spend some time in Paris. The abbot objected and claimed that his niece was under his protection. In fact, the unfortunate woman fell out of the frying pan into the fire, for on the return journey the abbot confessed his passion for her and, when she became indignant, began to persecute her ferociously. At Turin he turned husband and mother-in-law against her. "She suffered for a while longer, but virtue finally giving in to madness and bad domestic treatment, she at last listened to Monsieur de Savoie and gave herself to him in order to be free of persecution. Here is a real novel," concluded Saint-Simon, "but it occurred in our time to everybody's knowledge."

Mme. de Verrue was named lady of honor to the Duchess of Savoy and had a suite at the royal palace. She supported the French party against the Austrian influence. The duke fell passionately in love with her and, when she had smallpox, did not hesitate to remain with her and nurse her with his own hands. But he was suspicious, jealous and difficult. The young woman was forced into a sultana's existence and kept in the "seraglio." She consoled herself by collecting furniture, paintings and art objects. After ten years of this existence, she had enough. Taking advantage of Victor Amadeus' absence at Chambéry, she had transported into France the finest works of her collection, aided by her brother, the Chevalier de Luynes, and secretly crossed the frontier in October, 1700. According to Tessé, the Duke of Savoy was "quite piqued by this method"—and one can easily understand. He did not really care for her, only for the two children the countess had given him and whom he legitimatized in 1701. The son, Marquis de Susa, died without issue. The daughter married the Prince de Carignan of the youngest branch of the House of Savoy which in 1831 ascended the throne of Sardinia in the person of Charles Albert from whom the last king of Italy was directly descended.

*Charles-Emmanuel I*

Victor Amadeus, widower in 1728, remarried in 1729. His bride was Anne-Thérèse de Cumiane, forty-five years of age; she had been his mistress twenty-five years before when she was the maid of honor to Madama Reale. At this time, according to the words of a contemporary, the duke had "overwhelmed her with extraordinary gifts which soon distinguished her from her companions by rounding out her body to a considerable degree." In 1730 he abdicated in favor of his son Charles Emmanuel III and died two years later.

In 1805, during the annexation of Piedmont by France, Napoleon stayed at the royal palace. The governor of Piedmont was then the Prince Borghese, husband of Pauline Bonaparte, but the latter remained only for short periods at Turin. Victor Emmanuel I, King of Sardinia, regained his states in 1815. His brother Charles Felix succeeded him in 1831 and died childless. The crown of Italy then passed to Charles Albert of the Carignan branch, who in 1834 had Pelagio Palagi redecorate various rooms on the first floor of the palace. Then Victor Emmanuel inherited the crown, and when he chose Florence as his capital in 1865, the palace was inhabited only on rare occasions. The royal collection of paintings, which included Prince Eugene's famous collection acquired by Charles Emmanuel III in 1747, had been removed from the palace by 1832 to be exhibited at the Palazzo Madama. They can still be seen today at the Galleria Sabauda. The interior decoration and the furnishings, however, have remained almost intact. The palace now belongs to the Italian State.

## Isola Bella *Villa Borromeo*

Leaving his Montebello headquarters, Bonaparte landed on Isola Bella in August, 1797, a few months before the signing of the Treaty of Campo Formio. He was accompanied by the *citoyenne* Bonaparte, the Ambassador of the French Republic at the Court of Turin, General Louis Alexandre Berthier, and a suite of sixty-six persons. Their arrival aboard two gunboats appeared to the Borromeo superintendent who was about to receive them "as one of the finest sights he had ever witnessed . . ." A meal was served in the Medal Room and the superintendent related that "the general remained pensive, even at the table, yet affable and attentive, requesting news of the Borromeo family." Napoleon spent the night at the palace in a room which has remained the same since that day. He also visited Isola Madre, where he spent two hours admiring the breeding of pheasants and even requested that one of the birds be killed so that he could take it with him.

He was later to return to Isola Bella, this time as Emperor of the French and King of Italy. Prince Borromeo received him with magnificent receptions, although only shortly before the French troops had destroyed the Rocca d'Arona, the fortress which belonged to his family. A concert was held in the gardens, where the sublime Grassini, diva of La Scala, sang the favorite arias of the Emperor, who had adored her during their first meeting at Milan, asked her to come to Paris, then left her after a stormy liaison.

The first work destined for the arrangement of the isle and the erection of the palace was undertaken shortly after 1630 from the plans of Antonio Crivelli for Count Charles Borromeo. The isle was then known as Isola Isabella, in honor of Count Borromeo's wife, who owned not only the other Borromean isles but also vast domains in Ticino, Switzerland. The Borromeo were, in fact, a very powerful family and could pride themselves on Saint Charles Borromeo, one of the most eminent saints of the Counter-Reformation.

Gardens and villa were in an outline state when Charles Borromeo died. His son, Count Vitaliano, actively continued the work with the aid of a whole team of architects and sculptors. Barca laid out the gardens, which were finished in 1670. For the design of the palace, Vitaliano commissioned the great architect of pontifical Rome, Carlo Fontana, who furnished a grandiose project, left unfinished, but the achievement was continued by the present Prince Borromeo.

*Richard Wagner*

*La Grassini*

From the close of the seventeenth century down to modern times, the gardens inspired the most passionate remarks. "The Borromean Isles, in my opinion, are a real sojourn of Epicurus and Sardanapalus," wrote Charles de Brosses among other lyrical praise. "It is only with regret that one leaves this charming place," stated Montesquieu. And Goethe, it is said, was thinking of these isles when Mignon praises "the fabulous country where lemon trees blossom."

With Stendhal the tone changed: the site enchanted him. "The divine Borromean Isles seem to produce the feeling of beauty in a greater quantity than St. Peter's." The garden of Isola Bella, on the other hand, was only worthy of this scornful commentary: "Contemporary of Versailles. Greater for a private person than Versailles for a king but as dry for the heart as Versailles." Wagner showed greater taste. In *My Life* he described his visit here in the spring of 1852. "Shortly after sundown I saw the Borromean Isles gracefully emerge from the waves of the lake and I could not sleep for the joy the following day had to offer. On the morrow the visit enchanted me to the point where my delight was disturbing: I wondered how all this was possible and what I ought to do about it." Wagner later returned to the Borromean Isles during the summer of 1858, shortly after the tragedies created by the quarrels between his wife Minna and Mathilda Wesendonck. "There on the terraces of Isola Bella

*Count Vitaliano Borromeo*

in the company of my young friend (Carl Ritter), who was never indiscreet but rather too silent, I enjoyed a wonderful summer morning. For the first time after such a long period I felt utterly tranquil and began again to dream of a future of peace and harmony."

During the Belle Epoque the Borromean Isles became the ideal setting of every amorous exaltation, and in a famous novel René Boylesve evoked their intoxicating "perfume." It was in the palace which, in 1935, witnessed the Conference of Stresa between Italy, France and Britain that the integrity and independence of Austria were once again affirmed—three years before the Anschluss.

Isola Bella and the other Borromean Isles belong to Prince Vitaliano Borromeo.

## Stupinigi *Palazzina di Caccia*

It is Victor Amadeus II, Duke of Savoy, then King of Sardinia, to whom we are indebted for conceiving the plan of the Palazzina di Caccia—hunting pavilion—of Stupinigi in 1729. The design was requested from Filippo Juvara who drew it up in 1729-1730. Work was undertaken at once and actively carried out, since in 1731 the brothers Giuseppe and Domenico Valeriani executed the painted decoration of the great central salon. Victor Amadeus, however, was not destined to see the finished pavilion, for he had abdicated in 1730 in favor of his son Charles Emmanuel III. Shortly afterward he wanted to regain the crown and Charles Emmanuel had him interned at Moncalieri, where he died in 1732.

The gradual completion of the palace continued until the close of the eighteenth century. By 1729, even before Juvara's departure for Spain (1735), the direction of the work was entrusted to one of his pupils, Giovanni Tomaso Prunotto, who was dismissed from his duties in 1737, after the death of his master. But it appears that Juvara's initial project did not have the fullness of the present edifice. From a mere hunting pavilion—needless to say, already rather impressive considering the dimensions of the central salon—the Palazzina di Caccia became a veritable residence of the royal family. To hold the court and its suite, the main building was therefore enlarged, extending it by the wings which framed the cours d'honneur and its forecourts.

The interior decoration was entrusted to a whole team of painters, sculptors and gilders, including the Valeriani brothers, Giovanni Battista Crosato, the Viennese Wehrlin and Carle van Loo, who worked at Stupinigi in 1733. The gardens were designed by a Frenchman, François Bernard (his plans date from 1740).

The domain of the Palazzina was originally a part of the possessions of the Order of Saint Maurice and Saint Lazarus. The Order of Saint Maurice had been founded in 1434 by Amadeus VIII of Savoy (1383-1451), the future Pope Felix V. In 1572, the Duke Emmanuel Philibert obtained the authorization of Pope Gregory XIII to unite the Order of Saint Maurice and that of Saint Lazarus and presented them with the territory of Stupinigi. It was Victor Amadeus II, Grand Master of the Order, who, as we have seen, built the present castle.

In 1772, the administration of Stupinigi was entrusted to the royal treasury. During the Revolution, at the time of French occupation, the Order of Saint Maurice and of Saint Lazarus was suppressed, and for a while Stupinigi was ceded to the citizen Francesco Antonio Garda in payment of debts contracted by the government during the war. But by 1801 Garda exchanged Stupinigi for other lands also seized from the Order. In 1801 the domain was granted to the University of Turin. In 1803 Napoleon made it into one of his residences in Italy and spent the night in May, 1805, before his coronation at Milan as King of Italy. Pauline Borghese, whose husband Prince Camillo Borghese was governor of Piedmont, seldom came here but had it arranged for him, including the decoration of the bath-

*Victor Amadeus II*

room. After 1815, the House of Savoy regained possession of its properties. The marriage of Victor Emmanuel II and Maria Adelaide of Hapsburg was celebrated here in 1842 and that of their second son, the Duke of Aosta, who was to become King of Spain from 1870 to 1873, was also celebrated at the Palazzina. Queen Margaret, widow of King Humbert, resided here from 1900 to 1919.

In 1919 the Crown of Italy conceded Stupinigi to the Italian state, but in 1925 a royal decree returned the domain and the castle to the Order of Saint Maurice and Saint Lazarus, which continues to take great care of this splendid residence, its park and its museum of decorative art.

*Victor Emmanuel II as Grand Master of the Order of Saint Maurice*

# *Villa Carpeneto*

Turin

Reflecting its calm design in a mirror of water enamelled with water lilies, the villa *(above)* is a huge elongated construction enlivened by an extended central pavilion with a loggia. In its present state it dates from 1769-1770 and is the work of the architect Francesco Valeriano Dellala di Beinasco; but it replaced a seventeenth-century villa, itself erected on remains of a medieval fortress. The loggia *(left page)* is decorated with pilasters and light stucco arabesques as well as a superb wrought-iron fretworked lantern. It opens largely on the foliage of the park.

In the staircase *(below)* a shell with its subtle wavy design supports the landing of the first floor and forms the center of a composition consisting entirely of volutes and scrolls of remarkable elegance. Light mouldings and foliated motifs emphasize the spiral movement of the delicately worked wrought-iron banister. The staircase is topped by a vault arranged in a central oculus and adorned with fine stucco lacework.

In contrast with the subtle elegance of the staircase, the great central salon *(right page)* is in the severe neo-classic taste. Massive Corinthian pilasters rise to the very height of these two floors and support the coffer-decorated vault; alternately round and triangular pediments surmount doors and windows. This decoration of great nobility probably dates from the very close of the eighteenth century; it was entirely executed in *trompe-l'oeil*—even the cornice is an illusion. Following the Italian tradition, the huge room is plainly furnished with consoles and seats strictly aligned along the walls, in such a way as not to alter the architectural character of the design.

# *Palazzo Madama*

"The Palazzo Madama has a superb façade . . . we can even say that this façade is the chief ornament of the city," wrote the French historian, Charles de Brosses. "In the interior is one of the handsomest staircases in the world with its double flight of steps and adorned with fine architecture. . . . Do not look for more here: at the end of this there are no suites; it is a staircase without a palace." In fact although Charles de Brosses rather exaggerated—for the suites of the Palazzo Madama are important—the staircase and the façade *(left page and above)* are the most remarkable features: they were built from 1718 to 1721 from the design by Filippo Juvara. Bathed in light, the staircase with its double flight of steps is supported by vaults and columns of surprising lightness. The façade with its harmonious flow of Corinthian columns and pilasters, crowned by balustrades, statues and vases, was originally the core of a much more important composition. According to Juvara's design, two wings terminating in higher pavilions flanked it on both sides, but only the central part which concealed the older constructions was executed.

A respectable widow, as is evident from her full black headdress and the stiff small collar, but very fond of luxury and willingly elegant, as revealed by the pearls and the neck of her décolletage, Madame Royale *(above)* gave her name to the Palazzo Madama. Sister of Louis XIII, wife of Duke Victor Amadeus I, ruling in the name of her sons from 1637 to 1648, she had the old medieval palace completely remodelled so that it would be worthy of her rank as "daughter of France."

In a vertiginous flight, the angel of the Lord catches the arm of Abraham about to sacrifice his son Isaac *(right page)*. Executed in wood and ivory, this work by Simone Troger, which dates from 1734, is among the most remarkable in the Museo d'Arte Antica now contained in the Palazzo Madama. The very characteristic taste of eighteenth-century Italy for virtuosity and mastering difficulty is revealed here with a *maestria* which offers no surprise. There are other handsome ivories in the collection, including that of a faun, with a very expressive and realistically modeled mask, who is frantically striking his cymbals.

Turin

# *Royal Palace*

A marvel of technical virtuosity, the cupola of the Chapel of the Holy Shroud *(left page)* is supported by a drum with arcades and consists of a superposition of remarkably light open arcades, terminating in a central opening in the form of a star. The whole is 180 feet high. Begun in 1668 from the design by the Theatine monk Guarino Guarini (1624-1683), the chapel was not finished until after the death of the architect in 1694. It extended from the Cathedral of Saint John but found itself included in the construction of the royal palace. It was destined to contain—and still contains—the Holy Shroud brought to Turin in 1578 by the Duke Emmanuel Philibert. It was during this last transfer that Charles Borromeo made the journey on foot from Milan to Turin to venerate the holy relic.

Proudly caracolled on their rearing mounts, Castor and Pollux *(above)* guard the entrance to the palace and to the "piazza reale" facing it. Executed in 1846, they are the work of Abbondio Sangiorgio and date from the transformations of the edifice in the seventeenth century by Pelagio Palagi. At the far end, dominating the square, we see the dome of the Church of San Lorenzo, another achievement of unusual elegance by Father Guarini.

Glimmering in the soft glitter of its gold colors, the "alcove chamber," decorated about 1670, was originally the "state chamber" of Charles Emmanuel II, then used as the reception salon for the queens of Sardinia. It was here that Charles Albert kept his collection of Far Eastern porcelain which can still be seen. Figures of women emerge from sumptuously executed sheaths which separate the alcove of the chamber, stretched beneath a damask of faded delicate pinks and old gold. This superb decoration, designed by Carlo Morello, was executed in 1662-1663 by the woodcarvers Bartolomeo Botto, Emanuele and Francesco Dugar, and Quirino Castelli. The paintings which adorn the frieze are by Pierre Dufour and his brothers Laurent and Gabriel, while those above the doors are the work of Sebastiano Ricci. The portrait by Benvenuti above the console is that of Queen Maria Theresa, daughter of the Grand Duke of Tuscany, Ferdinand III, and wife of Charles Albert.

It was on the table in the salon of the ministers' council that, according to tradition, Charles Albert on March 4, 1848, signed the *Statuto,* the liberal constitution granted to the Kingdom of Sardinia, which included Piedmont, and subsequently became that of the Kingdom of Naples. The decoration of the salon and its furnishings were executed from the design by the Bolognese Pelagio Palagi, named in 1834 "painter appointed to decorate the royal palaces" and who then modified several rooms of the suites. The chairs and the table, with their rather heavy splendid ornamentation derived from the antique, are a late Italian interpretation of the French Empire style.

The portraits of the various members of the House of Savoy which cover the walls of the "cabinet of miniatures" *(above)* are integrated with a perfect decorative sense into the "mirror floors" which serve as their background and reflect them endlessly. The frames, the foundations, the pilasters and the inner shutters are entirely gilded. The carving of the wood panelling which, under French influence, Piedmont preferred to the stucco dear to eighteenth-century Italy, here achieves a finesse and delicacy so evident in the work of the goldsmiths of the period.

In the domain of interior decoration the Chinese cabinet *(left page)* is no doubt one of Filippo Juvara's most brilliant achievements. Finely carved red and gold framework heightens the dark gleam of the lacquered panels, while the marble of the fireplace resumes with extreme subtlety the colored harmony of the mural decoration. Following a tradition well established in the eighteenth century, a delightful "chinoiserie" obstructs the foyer which is only discovered when the fire is lit. The floor is decorated with a geometric mosaic pattern that forms a pleasant contrast with the exuberance of the wood panelling and the fireplace.

# *Villa Borromeo*

"This resembles nothing but an enchanted palace," wrote Charles de Brosses in regard to Isola Bella. "This site is worthy of fairies. One would think they had brought here that section of the ancient Garden of Hesperides." Spread out in a series of terraces which descend toward Lake Maggiore, the gardens, begun shortly before 1630, were finished in 1670 from the design by the architect Barca for the prince Vitaliano Borromeo. The flowerbeds are a capricious lacework of arabesques of box trees, guarding the statues erected on the stone balustrades. The gleam of the water endows this sumptuous design with an air of calm and peace.

Floating on the lake like a mysterious apparition, the isle recalls the time when Armida kept Renaldo a prisoner in Ariosto's *Orlando Furioso*. The snow-capped mountains which break up the horizon intensify the sense of enchantment. Colossal foundations support nine terraces laid out in tiers. Pines, cypresses and clumps of trees arranged like huge bouquets of foliage frame the statues, the balustrades and the obelisks, and offer their rustic charm to this enterprise entirely achieved by the hand of man.

Frozen in postures of delirious abandon, an entire world of statues, gods, goddesses and *putti* on the summit of the island inhabit an architecture of rockwork dominated by a rider galloping a unicorn. Slender obelisks topped by panaches give harmony to the composition and provide a static element to this ensemble of exacerbated Baroque. The grottoes covered with stone are spread out on a concave plan and framed by an artificial lake with a white peacock as the miraculous bird of this enchanting décor.

# *Palazzina di Caccia*

The central pavilion of the Palazzina contains a splendid ballroom *(left page and above)* entirely painted in *trompe-l'œil* by the brothers Giuseppe and Domenico Valeriani in 1731. Oval in plan, it is crowned by a vault supported by four pillars which delimit four semicircular apses. A balcony with undulating lines, supported by massive consoles, encircles the room at the height of the first floor. The superb decoration, perfectly balanced in a powerful Baroque style, was devoted to the hunting exploits of the kings of Sardinia, evoked by a series of brackets surmounted by antlers.

Juvara's sketch *(right)* gives a very exact idea of the plan of the ensemble of the edifice as it was carried out *(following double page)*: four main buildings forming a cross of Saint Andrew emerging from an oval central pavilion, made higher and crowned by a gored dome, which dominates the composition. On the entrance side, two of the arms of the cross are extended by much lower wings which define a huge octagonal cours d'honneur. The beauty of the ensemble stems from the clarity of the plan and the perfect equilibrium of the volume which, thanks to the play of light, are splendidly arranged to create an astonishing impression of life and movement. Begun in 1729, the edifice was not finished until the close of the eighteenth century, long after Juvara's death. The stag which crowns the central pavilion recalls the original purpose of the palace, that of a hunting pavilion, which finally acquired the dimensions of a real royal residence.

Grimacing figures arranged in the landscape according to the laws of Far Eastern perspective, which are strict in spite of their apparent liberty, adorn the wallpaper of the Chinese Room *(opposite)* dating from the latter half of the eighteenth century.

The library *(above)* consists of two huge rooms covered with paned bookcases with wooden paneling dating from the middle of the eighteenth century. French influence can be seen in the design of the pilasters which create a rhythmic arrangement, although the busy door pediment and the style of the ornament are characteristic of the Rococo taste of Piedmont.

卦
命
官

# *Venetia*

*With its back to Lake Garda and the Alps, bordered by the Po but largely open to the Adriatic, Venetia was the heart of a state whose force and wealth dominated Mediterranean history in the Middle Ages. Venice, the most powerful city of medieval Europe, created a real empire without submitting to a dynasty. Corfu, Crete and Cyprus as well as many Adriatic ports were stopping places for the Venetian galleys which sailed as far as Egypt, to the mouth of the Don, to Syria and other Eastern lands, or steered their course toward the Atlantic to trade in the Netherlands and England.*

*As early as the fifteenth century Frioul, Istria, Dalmatia, Treviso, Padua and Vicenza came under the domination of Venice, thus adding an important land domain to her maritime empire. With the completion of the Doges' Palace and of the Piazza San Marco, and with the flowering of one of the greatest schools of painting, from Bellini to Titian, the splendor of Venice reached its zenith. The decline of the Republic was first felt after the discovery of the maritime route to the Indies and it was to become irremediable in the eighteenth century. The Republic was in its last throes, although retaining an amazing degree of luxury, when Napoleon gave Austria the territory of Venice as far as the Adige in the Treaty of Campo Formio. Her artistic glory, however, remained and the splendor of her palaces inspired many artists and writers to settle in the city.*

Venice

## *Palazzo Albrizzi*

On November 7, 1920, shortly after Countess Elsa Albrizzi's death, Gabriele D'Annunzio, then in Fiume, wrote to the late Countess's daughter: "I can only think that, if I return to Venice, I will no longer find the sweet face of the woman who for me on every occasion was the most faithful friend. I am thinking again of our musical evenings, the wood burning in the fireplace, the narrow table, of so many sweet and profound things, now abolished by the cruelty of life, of the trellis of the intimate garden gradually bared of its leaves. Give an occasional thought to your poor martyred friend."

In fact, Countess Elsa Albrizzi had often held musical evenings, whose "charm and beauty" the poet had enjoyed, and took pleasure in gathering around her artists, literary men and diplomats, including Ottorino Respighi, Pompeo Molmenti and Constantino Nigra. Actually she was merely resuming a tradition well established at the Palazzo Albrizzi. At the beginning of the nineteenth century Countess Isabella Teotochi-Albrizzi had presided over the most important salon in Venice, renowned for its liberal ideals and frequented by Count Vittorio Alfieri, Ugo Foscolo, Ippolito Pindemonte and Count Cicognara, president of the Academy of Fine Arts, and where Chateaubriand, Mme. de Staël and Sir Walter Scott were received.

*Countess Isabella Teotochi Albrizzi*

Born at Corfu, she had been married at a young age to a Teotochi from whom she soon separated. Later she married Count Albrizzi Sismondi, who was much enamored of her. He described her as "a woman who brings honor to Greece where she was born and to Italy where she lives; every poet has sung her praises, every literary man has been enthusiastic over her and anyone who has seen her has adored her." The celebrated sculptor, Antonio Canova, executed a bust of Helen of Troy which, in fact, is her portrait and can still be seen in the palace. It was in her salon that Byron met Countess Guiccioli. When the poet left for Rome in 1817, Isabella Albrizzi gave him a letter of introduction to Canova. "To the famous name of Lord Byron and the admiration aroused on reading his work," she wrote, "I will add the greatest charm and the most delightful conversation which I often had the honour of enjoying in his company. During these discussions the name of Canova was often mentioned associated with that of the 'Helen.' He has composed a very fine epigram on the beautiful Greek woman who at present is said to be rather the work of Canova than of Homer."

The friendship between Isabella and Byron, however, lasted only a short time. Isabella had created a series of *ritratti* or brief literary portraits of her friends, written in a very lively style—and apparently with kindness toward them uppermost in her thoughts. She wanted to add that of the young poet and, requesting his permission, offered to read her text to him. But Byron preferred to create his personality and legend himself, not only in the eyes of his contemporaries but in those of posterity as well. He declined the offer and stated quite frankly that the greatest pleasure the author could give him would be to burn these pages at once. The countess, however, did not bear him any ill will in another "portrait" of him written after his death, in 1826. As for Byron, he preferred to withdraw from the "finest" of Venetian society in 1818 to frequent the more mingled and less restricted society, morally speaking, of Countess Marina Benzon who, more than sixty years of age, was enamored of him to the point "of making herself ridiculous in ecstasies of joy."

The Palazzo Albrizzi, one of the most perfectly preserved in Venice, was begun at the close of the sixteenth century by the Bonomo family. The Albrizzi acquired a part—the "piano nobile" or noble story—in 1648, and completed their purchase in 1692. Natives of Bergamo, like most Venetian families they had become wealthy trading with the Middle East and were admitted to the Grand Council in 1667. Of the inner decoration dating from the sixteenth century there remains only the great entrance hall. During the last quarter of the seventeenth century and the first half of the eighteenth, the salons were magnificently decorated with stucco. Several were once again redecorated at the close of the eighteenth century. The second floor was finally decorated in the Pompeian style from 1800 to 1825, especially by Borsato. Since that period the palace and its furnishings have scarcely been modified. On August 10, 1916, an Austrian bomb fell on the edifice but fortunately did not explode. For the plaque placed on the palace to mark the event, D'Annunzio composed a stigmatizing inscription. "This mark of barbarism embedded in stone denounces the eternal enemy who thus adds new shame to his shame, new glory to our glory."

The palace—the only one along with the Palazzo Donà dalle Rose to have remained in the hands of the same family since the seventeenth century—now belongs to Baron and Baroness Rubin de Cervin Albrizzi who preserve and maintain their magnificent dwelling with the greatest care.

## Padua *Palazzo Frigimelica-Selvatico*

*The tempestuous Charlotte Aglae d'Orléans*

By the close of the fourteenth century the Frigimelica possessed a dwelling on the site of the present palace, in via dei Tadi, according to the will drawn up in 1428 by Francesco Frigimelica, who mentioned a "casa grande" as part of his possessions. The Frigimelica belonged to a very ancient family; as early as the eleventh century one of its members was mentioned in regard to a donation made by Orlando, a descendant of Charlemagne. In the sixteenth and seventeenth centuries we find them listed as professors of medicine and philosophy at the famous University of Padua. Francesco Frigimelica was chief physician to Pope Julius III.

In its present state the most ancient sections of the palace do not date later than the sixteenth century. In fact, it was entirely remodelled and enlarged between 1660 and 1683, then modified once again from 1776 to 1793. During this last period, from 1778 to 1781, the decoration of the apartments was also renovated.

In 1786 the palace passed by maternal descent into the hands of the Selvatico. Originally from Milan, the Selvatico family had settled in Padua in 1310. It was distinguished for its warriors, its professors at the University, notably Benedetto Selvatico (1575-1658), chief physician to Emperor Ferdinand III, and its diplomats. In 1719 Benedetto Selvatico (1666-1741) was sent to France by the Duke of Modena, Renaud d'Este, in order to escort Mademoiselle de Valois, the Regent's daughter, on her trip to Modena for her marriage to the heir to the throne, Francesco Maria d'Este. A delicate mission considering the bride's character! Her liaison with the Duc de Richelieu at the time of her engagement caused a scandal. "Unfortunately, it was an open secret why the Regent rid himself of the Princess—and with so little discernment," says Saint-Simon. According to contemporary lampoons the princess was furious at the thought of going to "the sad site of Modena" and of leaving "Richelieu" behind in Paris. An opportune case of measles broke out the day after her marriage by proxy. She finally had to leave but the journey was made in small stages and as slowly as possible. The Duke of Modena was furious and we can imagine Selvatico's situation.

In 1797 Napoleon, passing through Padua, spent the night at the palace. In 1949 the Selvatico sold their dwelling and since that date it has been wonderfully restored and decorated with handsome eighteenth-century furnishings, the majority Venetian, and several once contained in the Palazzo Labia.

*Marquis Benedetto Selvatico received by Louis XV*

Vicenza

# *Villa Valmarana dei Nani*

The villa consists of several buildings: the principal edifice reserved for the owners and known as the "casa padronale," the guest house or "foresteria," the stables, outbuildings and others. The principal residence was begun in 1669 by Antonio Muttoni for the jurisconsult Bertolo. Francesco Muttoni, Antonio's son, built the "foresteria" and the stables in the early eighteenth century. The villa was acquired in the mid-eighteenth century by the Valmarana family who, in 1757, commissioned Gianbattista Tiepolo and his son Giandomenico to decorate the "casa padronale" and the "foresteria," and the frescoes executed by father and son are superb. Goethe, who saw them during his journey to Italy, wrote (he probably did not know that they had not all been painted by Gianbattista): "Today I saw the Villa Valmarana which Tiepolo decorated, giving free play to all his qualities and all his faults. He is less successful with the sublime style than with a natural one. But in the present case I have

*Villa Valmarana*

seen some superb things. As a decorator, on the whole, he has much genius and imagination." Perhaps it is at the Villa Valmarana in this exquisitely fanciful decoration that we can best imagine the *villeggiatura* praised by Carlo Goldoni:

*Everyone enjoys complete freedom.*
*Sleeps he who wants, eats he who is hungry,*
*Dances he who wants to dance, sings he who is able to.*
*One man goes for a solitary walk in the gardens,*
*The other goes there accompanied by ladies. . . .*

Since the eighteenth century the villa has remained in the hands of the Valmarana family.

## Stra *Villa Pisani*

In *Il Fuoco* (1900)—translated into English as *The Flame of Life*—Gabriele D'Annunzio described the automobile trip which took his hero Stelio Effrena and his mistress, the great actress Foscarina, along the Brenta River to Stra. (The novel is partly autobiographical, the character of Foscarina being based on Éleanora Duse, with whom D'Annunzio had had a love affair.) "They drove up in front of the villa of the Pisani, entered and accompanied by a guardian, visited the empty apartments. They could hear the sound of their steps on the reflecting marble, the echo in the historiated vaults, the fastidious voice awakening memories. . . . 'This room is that of the Emperor,' said the guardian solemnly as he opened both leaves of a door. . . . The great shadow seemed omnipresent in the villa of doge Alvise. The imperial eagles, emblems of his power, dominated from above all the pale relics. But in this yellow room the shadow covered the huge bed, fell beneath the canopy between the four columns surmounted by golden flames. The formidable sigla inscribed in the crown of laurels glittered on the bed head. And this kind of funerary layer was continued in the mirror between two victories supporting the candelabra."

The first projects destined to replace the villa which the Pisani had at Stra since the sixteenth century were requested about 1730 by Alvise Pisani (1664-1741) from the architect Girolamo Frigimelica. In the Correr Museum there is a wooden model of the proposed building which was never constructed. Although the adjoining buildings were executed from the designs by Frigimelica, who died in 1732, the villa itself is the work of Maria Preti.

Alvise Pisani belonged to a family mentioned in notary deeds as early as 1228 and who entered the Grand Council under the dogeship of Pietro Gradenigo (1289-1311). During the period of their power, genealogists enjoyed tracing their origin to Calpurnius, the son of Numa Pompilius. Alvise had embarked upon a diplomatic career with an ostentation that gained him the reputation "of taking with him the entire majesty of the Venetian senate." In 1698 he was named ambassador to France—Louis XIV was godfather of one of his sons—then ambassador to England. On his return to Venice, he held several important posts. Elected doge in 1735, he was prudent enough to refuse joining Austria against the Turks, a measure which would have ruined Venetian trade in the Levant at a period when the decline of the Republic was already well advanced. Even more than his outstanding political qualities, it was his elegance, his love of luxury, the splendor of his residences at Stra and Venice, at the Palazzo Pisani, of Campo San Stefano (today Liceo Musicale Benedetto Marcello), that dazzled his contemporaries.

The villa at Stra remained in his family—the male line of which died out about 1750—until 1807. It was then acquired by Napoleon who in November of that year spent the night on his way from Padua to Venice. Charles IV, the dethroned king of Spain, Queen Maria Louisa of Parma and her lover, Manuel de Godoy, Prince of the Peace—a strange combination of three old persons termed by the queen herself as "Trinity on Earth"—resided here for some time in 1817. During the annexation of Venetia by the kingdom of Italy, the villa became royal property. At the present time the villa belongs to the Italian State.

*Admiral Angelo Emo*

## Venice *Palazzo Treves de' Bonfilii*

In 1828 the Venetians were upset by the arrival at the Palazzo Treves de' Bonfilii of two enormous cases, but their surprise gave way to joy and pride when they learned that these contained the two colossal statues of Hector and Ajax, the work of Antonio Canova, which had apparently vanished six years previously. It was only with the greatest difficulty that Baron Treves de' Bonfilii had gained possession of the two statues which had remained in the sculptor's studio in Rome after his death and had been inexplicably overlooked. To transport these two enormous sculptures from Rome to Venice had posed many problems. The statues were sent by land on a wagon drawn by oxen, the journey taking six months. They were finally placed in the salon specially arranged for them. Emperor Ferdinand of Austria, who had come to Venice for his coronation in October, 1836, made a special visit to admire them, accompanied by the Empress and the Archduke Rénier, governor of Lombardia-Venetia, an event which the artist Borsato commemorated in a charming small painting now kept in the palace.

In the Middle Ages, on the site of the

present Palazzo Treves de' Bonfilii, there already existed a Gothic fortress belonging to the Barozzi, which protected the entrance to the Grand Canal. It is indicated on the topographical map of Venice which was executed about 1500 and attributed to Albrecht Dürer. There remains a tower englobed in subsequent constructions. The Barozzi belonged to one of the oldest Venetian families, and Andrea Barozzi, captain general of the Republic's fifty-five galleys, distinguished himself in 1264 in a naval combat against the

*Admiral Angelo Emo*

Genoese. In the early seventeenth century the Barozzi entirely rebuilt their dwelling. The façade on the San Moisè Canal is attributed both to the architect Bartolomeo Monopola and to Baldasarre Longhena. Later the palace passed by marriage into the hands of the Correr family; then in the eighteenth century it was acquired by the Emo-Capodilista. The great admiral Angelo Emo (1731-1792) resided here. In the early nineteenth century the poetess Giustina Renier Michiel, patrician of Venice and author of the *Feste Veneziane*, had a suite in the palace, which was sold in 1827 by Giorgio Emo-Capodilista, archbishop of Corfu, to Baron Giacomo Treves de' Bonfilii.

Baron Giacomo Treves de' Bonfilii belonged to a family whose members began to make a name for themselves about 1650, as a result of their activities as ship owners dealing with the East and America. In the early nineteenth century Giuseppe Treves de' Bonfilii enjoyed an important political and social position, especially after he was named by Napoleon baron of the kingdom of Naples. His son, Baron Jacopo, showed a strong interest in the fine arts and was a member of the Academy presided over by his friend, Count Leopoldo Cicognara, to whom Chateaubriand stated: "I am happy to contemplate the man who has given back Venice her life."

Baron Giacomo Treves de' Bonfilii had acquired, at the same time as the ancient Palazzo Barozzi, an adjoining house known as the Casa Zucchelli, and he commissioned the architect Meduna to join both buildings. The design of the salons was entrusted to a team of Venetian artists.

The palace, which has remained unchanged since that period, is now the property of the descendants of Baron Giacomo Treves de' Bonfilii.

Padua

## *Palazzo Emo Capodilista*

In the courtyard of the Palazzo Emo Capodilista can still be seen the cornel tree planted in 1194 by the blessed Giordano Forzatè, a member of the famous Forzatè family, to whom the Capodilista were related. The tree originally stood in the nearby convent of Saint Benedict, and was transplanted to its present site when the convent was secularized in the early nineteenth century. According to legend, one of its palms withers each time a death occurs in the family, which, it is said, will last as long as the tree blossoms.

The palace is the work of the Capodilista who, according to the ancient chronicles, are the descendants of two brothers, Giovanni and Carlotto, who came from Italy with Charlemagne to fight Didier, king of the Lombards, in 775. After the defeat of Didier, as a reward for their services, the Emperor presented them with the counties of Mandria and Piove di Sacco, the Castle of Montemerlo and territories beyond the Salgardo Mountains. Because of the latter gifts, Carlotto took the name of Transalgardi, while Giovanni founded the Forzatè—from *Sforza Tadi*, "victors over the Tadi," the Knights he had defeated in combat. One of Giovanni's nephews is responsible for the branch of the family which took the name of Capodilista.

The Forzatè held important posts at Padua since the most ancient period. The Blessed Giordano distinguished himself early in his career not only by his saintliness but also by his determination to support a relentless struggle against a certain Losco Transalgardino, leader of the city's popular party. In 1174, during a street fight, the latter set fire to the Forzatè dwelling and the conflagration spread so rapidly that it destroyed more than 2,000 houses. Fleeing the flames, Giordano Forzatè fell unconscious before the door of a small oratory, dedicated to Saint Benedict, which stood at the city gates. According to legend he was honored by a celestial vision which determined his conversion. He entered the Benedictine Order and undertook the construction of a more important monastery. Nevertheless, he continued to play a leading role in Paduan political life, distinguishing himself not only for his bravery but also for his wisdom and moderation. He refused the bishopric of Ferrara which had been offered him, used his influence to support Saint Anthony of Padua and adopted a heroic attitude toward Pope Ezzelino IV after the latter had seized control of Padua in 1237. He first sought refuge at the Castle of Montemerlo which belonged to his family, then, informed of the extortions demanded by the guilty tyrant, he decided to leave his place of safety and return to Padua. On arrival he presented himself to Ezzelino who immediately had him imprisoned in the dungeons of San Zeno. Only the intervention of Emperor Frederick II obtained his release. He retired to Venice and died there shortly afterward.

Although subsequently modified, the tower of the Palazzo Emo Capodilista, which dated from the close of the twelfth century, and the palace itself were erected during the Blessed Giordano's lifetime. The Capodilista continued to hold important positions at Padua, some notably at the University as jurisconsults. In 1434 Giovanni Francesco Capodilista drew up the Codice Capodilista (now in the Paduan library) which related the outstanding achievements of the family's most famous members, together with splendid miniature portraits. In 1433 he had been Pope Martin V's ambassador to the Council of Basle and on this occasion received from the Emperor Sigismond the title of Count and the right to include in his coat-of-arms the imperial eagle. He later represented Pope Eugene IV at the court of the same Emperor who granted him the privilege during his funeral to carry the imperial sceptre. During a parade in one of the streets of Padua in 1466, he caused a sensation by appearing followed by a figure of Jupiter on horseback entirely covered with gold and precious stones, the work of Donatello. The framework of the horse stood for a long time at the Palazzo Capodilista, where it was seen by Vasari, who wrote: "In the house of a Count Capodilista, he (Donatello) worked at the framework of a wooden horse which can still be seen but without its head. The framework is so perfect that anyone who considers this work can judge the resources of his imagination and the grandeur of his intelligence." The horse with its rebuilt head was later offered to the city of Padua along with other works of art and a collection of 543 paintings owned by Count Leonardo Emo Capodilista. These can now be seen at the Palazzo della Ragione and at the city museum.

*Giovanni Francesco Capodilista*

*The Blessed Giordano Forzate*

In the seventeenth century the Palazzo Capodilista underwent transformation designed to make it more livable. The ancient buildings were equipped with large windows and new constructions were added. In addition, the interior decoration was largely refurbished in the eighteenth century by Antonio Capodilista.

The palace was acquired by the Emo family when Beatrice, the last of the Capodilista, married Leonardo Emo in 1783. He belonged to one of the oldest Venetian families. According to ancient chronicles, it was originally from Greece and had established itself at Venice as early as 997. In 1122 Giovanni and Rigo Emo were mentioned on the occasion of an exemption privilege granted by the Doge Domenico Michiel to the city of Bari. In 1297, the Emo were inscribed in the Golden Book of Venetian nobility. They gave the Republic a great number of statesmen, bishops, magistrates, sea captains and ambassadors. In 1711 Giovanni Emo was sent to Versailles in an attempt, as Saint-Simon related, "to patch up the misunderstanding caused by the choice of Cardinal Ottoboni, a Venetian, as French Protector at Rome, and the exception he had made in his country's laws, but the business was not quite ripe and he returned unsuccessful." He was later ambassador in London and in Constantinople and in 1723 procurator of Saint Mark. Cardinal de Bernis, who knew him at Venice, mentioned him as one of the most popular figures of the Republic.

*Pentesilea, Countess Capodilista*

But the most famous member of the family was certainly Angelo Emo (1731-1792), the last Venetian admiral. Early in his career, he completed his education by a series of journeys, including one to Berlin, where he was presented to Frederick II with whom he had an amusing discussion. The Prussian king maintained that a fort well equipped with arms and ammunition had nothing to fear from a naval attack, while Emo stated that a fleet with heavy artillery could destroy the fort. The King became so excited that while gesticulating he came closer and closer to Emo who gradually stepped backward until he found himself against the wall. Interrupting Frederick he exclaimed: "Well, Majesty, I am now at the wall of the fort." And both broke out in laughter. In 1785 he led an expedition against the Berbers, bombarded Sousse and Sfax, and almost destroyed La Goulette completely. It appears that he wanted to go ahead and conquer Algeria and Tunisia to put an end to piratical activities, but the Republic's timid policy prevented him from carrying out his plan. He died in 1792, a few years before the fall of Venice. The city's leaders commissioned Canova to erect a funerary monument which can now be seen in the Arsenal Museum. In 1784 Ippolito Pindemonte dedicated a sonnet to him, which reads in part:

*Thanks to you, Emo, the sovereign lion of the Adriatic,*
*Awakened from a deep sleep, has raised its head.*
*To its ships is opened*
*The stormy ocean route.*

The Palazzo Emo Capodilista now belongs to a descendant of Leonardo Emo and Beatrice Capodilista.

Marcantonio Barbaro *by Tintoretto*

## Maser *Villa Barbaro*

Venetian ambassadors to Catherine de' Medici during the height of the Wars of Religion, Marcantonio Barbaro, for whom the Villa was built, left a curious picture of the state of anxiety in which the French court then found itself (November 18, 1562): "Things are happening here under the cloak of mysterious fear. No one's projects and plans are known. It seems in a way that each member of the Council has his own plan which he keeps to himself. It is obvious that the Guise and the Connétable have joined forces and the Queen seems to have great faith in Guise. But the truth is that her Majesty's wavering goes to the extreme and that from one hour to the next she conceives of new plans. And from morning to night she changes her plans three times a day. Yesterday morning she was at the Château de Madrid, than came to dine in Paris. She then considered going to the Pont de Charenton, but later changed her mind and went to the Bois de Vincennes. Such is the course of events. No one at court knows which decision to make."

Marcantonio Barbaro and his brother Daniele were members of a very old family which as early as the ninth century held important posts in Venice. In 1125, an ancestor, Marco Barbaro, *provveditore* of the fleet, distinguished himself in a combat against the Turks. As an Infidel was about to board the galley under his command, he ran him through with his sword. Than, unrolling the white turban from the Turk's head, he drew a circle on the cloth with the tip of his sword covered with his victim's blood. Henceforth this emblem was to serve as the family's coat-of-arms.

As noted before, Marcantonio Barbaro was Ambassador to the court of France, from 1561 to 1564, and negociated a loan of 100,000 *écus* which Catherine de' Medici was anxious to obtain from the Venetian Republic.

His reports relate the chief events which heighten the history of France at that period, including the siege of Bourges, the capture of Lyons by the Protestants, that of Orléans by Condé, the Toulouse riots, the assassination of Guise by Poltrot de Méré and the departure of the French bishops for the Council of Trent. At his departure, he was made a knight by Charles IX at Lyons. In 1568 he was named ambassador to Constantinople and for a short time was imprisoned during the war between the Sultan and the league formed by the Pope, Philip II of Spain and Venice. After the victory of Lepanto, he was entrusted with the task of negotiating peace. He later held various posts at Venice, reforming the University of Padua, presiding at the reconstruction of the Rialto Bridge and as *provveditore* general of the Frioul fortifying Palma. In 1574, he was one of the procurators entrusted with carrying the parasol during the receptions given in honor of Henry III. He died in 1595.

The Villa Barbaro like the nearby Tempietto was erected about 1560, from a design by Palladio who published it in his *I Quattro Libri dell' Architettura.* Owing to Marcantonio's frequent travels during this period, it was his brother Daniele who supervised the work. After serving as ambassador to England from 1548 to 1550, Daniele Barbaro joined the Church and was named Patriarch of Aquileia by Pope Julius III.

A man of great culture, a friend of Cardinal Bembo, Tasso and Aretino, the author of a *Commentary* on Aristotle's *Rhetorics* and of a *Dialogue on Eloquence,* he was particularly attracted to architecture. He has left us a translation of Vetruvius with heavy scholarly notes and a treatise on perspective. The credit was very probably his for choosing Palladio, whom he mentioned in his will as "our beloved architect" and to whom he left fifteen ducats—a modest sum, but he had long abandoned all he possessed to his brother. It was also he who commissioned Veronese and Alessandro Vittoria to execute the marvelous decoration of the villa and its gardens.

Daniele Barbaro *by Veronese*

After the death of Marcantonio Barbaro, the villa passed into the hands of his son, then through heritage to the Trevisan, the Basadonna, and about 1700 to the Manin—the family who gave Venice her last doge. The Manin sold it to the Giacomelli in 1840, then in 1934 Guiseppe Volpi, Count of Misurata, acquired it and left it in his will to his daughter Matina, Countess Luling Buschetti, the present owner of the Villa Barbaro. Thanks to opportune restoration work, she has been able to recreate its past splendor.

Venice

# *Palazzo Donà dalle Rose*

On April 17, 1606, after a heated consistory, Pope Paul V fulminated a monitory addressed to the Republic of Venice. The doge Leonardo Donà dalle Rose, who had been elected on the previous January 10, and the members of the Senate were threatened with excommunication if they failed to obey the pontifical orders within twenty-four days; three days after the expiration of the required time every Venetian citizen would be placed under an interdict. These severe measures marked the culmination of the struggles which had set Venice against the Holy See since the preceding year, when the Republic had arrested, judged and condemned to prison two priests accused of rapine, homicide and immoral offense without referring the matter to Rome. The Pope refused to accept what he considered a blow at ecclesiastical privileges. Venice considered the attitude of the Holy See an interference in state affairs; later the doge and the Senate even prohibited the establishment of a monastery or a church without their organization.

Far from allowing herself to be intimidated by the threat of interdict, the Republic expressly refused to yield to the Pope's orders, and Capuchins, Theatines and Jesuits who would not conduct religious services were expelled. Henri IV finally offered to act as mediator; negotiations were conducted by the French ambassador Alincourt and completed by the Cardinal de Joyeuse on April 21, 1607. The Papacy finally withdrew its charges and renounced most of its claims.

The firm attitude on the part of the doge Leonardo Donà dalle Rose (1536-1612) was chiefly responsible for the victory gained by the Republic. He had been ardently supported by his great friend Fra Paolo Sarpi (1552-1623). A Servite theologian, Fra Paolo distinguished himself by the research which earned him a reputation as one of the most universal minds of his time. Natural sciences (twenty years before William Harvey he was aware of the principle of blood circulation), magnetic phenomena and algebra successively drew his attention; he also aided Galileo, whom he called his father and master, in his astronomical observations. In 1606, he was appointed the theological consultor of the Republic, whose interests he strongly defended. His *Treatise on Interdict,* in particular, was a strong attack on the pontifical measures.

It is to Fra Paolo Sarpi that we attribute the design of the Palazzo Donà dalle Rose, undertaken by the doge Leonardo on the Fondamente Nuove in 1610. The doge belonged to one of the oldest Venetian families, originally from Byzantium, which has been represented in the Grand Council from the time of its creation in 1143. The family divided into two branches: the Donà dalle Rose and the Donà dalle Tresse. The first, to which the doge Leonardo belonged, had already given Venice the doge Francesco Donà who was elected in 1545 and ruled until he died in 1553. To the second branch belonged the doge Niccolò Donà who ruled but thirty-four days in 1618. During its long history both branches furnished the Republic with a great number of ambassadors, statesmen, bishops and admirals.

The doge Leonardo, who was unmarried, intended the palace for himself and his brother Niccolò and subsequently for his nephews. Leonardo's projects were grandiose, Niccolò's more modest and prudent, and discussions soon arose between the brothers on the subject of the expenses involved in the work. Some commentators attribute the sudden death of the doge on July 16, 1612, after a collegial meeting during which he had spoken with his usual zeal and eloquence, to these disagreements.

He left his fortune and his palace in trust to his nephews, Niccolò's sons. The palace was soon finished, the grandiose initial plans having been somewhat reduced. Since that time it has constantly remained along with its furnishings and its precious objects of art in the hands of Niccolò Donà's descendants and now belongs to Count Lorenzo Donà dalle Rose.

## Vicenza *Villa Rotonda*

"The site is among the most pleasant and delightful that one can imagine," Palladio wrote in his *I Quattro Libri dell'Architettura* in reference to the Rotonda erected from his design, "since it is situated on a hill easy to reach, bathed on one side by a navigable river, the Bacchiglione, and on the other, surrounded by pleasant hills forming a kind of vast theater. These hills are cultivated and produce an abundance

*Villa Rotonda*

of excellent fruit and very fine vineyards. That is why in order to enjoy these wonderful views from every point —some limited views, others more distant, and still others continuing to the horizon line—I have designed porticoes on the four sides of the edifice."

Palladio was commissioned to design the Villa Rotonda by the canon Paolo Almerico, referendary of popes Pius IV and Pius V, about 1550-1551. The construction for the most part was probably finished in 1553 when the canon received Marquise Lucrezia of Gonzaga-Manfrone. According to the chronicler Ruscelli the fête ended in fireworks: "After dinner in the company of a fine and very noble group of lords and gentle ladies, one could see rising from the neighboring hills a fire composed of innumerable fireworks which in a very attractive manner, very well arranged, rose to the sky."

On the death of Palladio in 1580, however, the work was not completely finished. When the canon Almerico died, his natural son sold the villa in 1591 to Odorico Capra, "condottiere of the Republic of Venice," and to his brother Mario. To finish the edifice, these two turned to Vincenzo Scamozzi. There has been much discussion on the importance of the modifications made by Scamozzi to the original plans. And the problem is all the more complex since Palladio's description in *I Quattro Libri dell'Architettura* does not correspond exactly to the vertical sections included in the same work. The description makes no mention of the attic story above the porticoes, a story which is quite evident in the vertical section. It is assumed that this story did not exist in the early stage of execution, the four porticoes delimiting, around the central cupola, four terraces above the noble story. Later Palladio may have modified his plan by adding the attic story.

Toward the middle of the nineteenth century the villa and the surrounding land were sold by the Capra and passed into the hands of various owners until 1911 when they were acquired by the Valmarana family. Long left in a state of abandonment, the edifice was in disastrous condition. After the first indispensable restoration work, the villa was occupied on several occasions by the army from 1915 to 1918, then by the Germans during World War II. Count Andrea di Valnière, the present owner, has restored the villa perfectly.

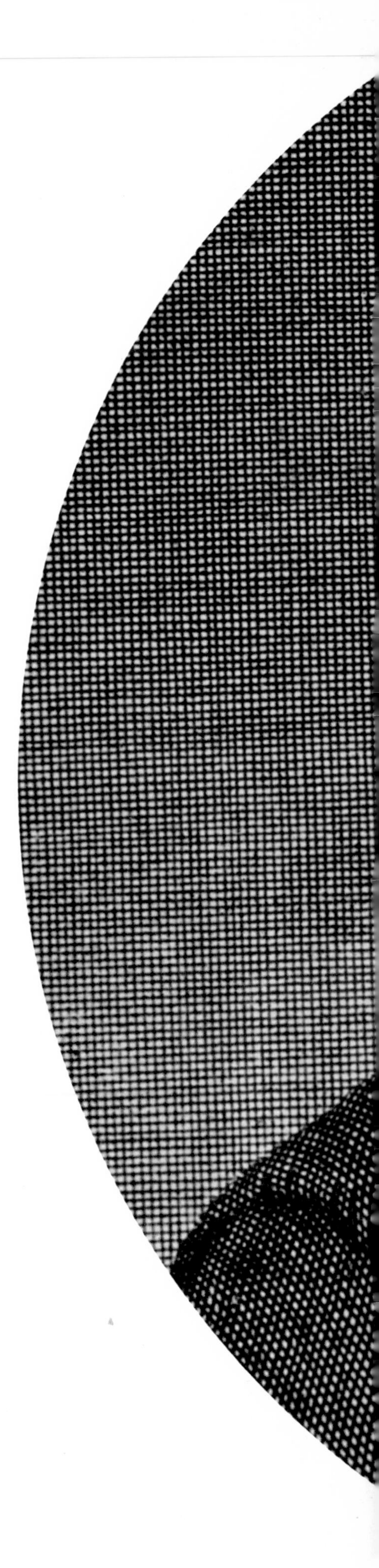

*Andrea Palladio*

# *Palazzo Albrizzi*

Venice

A bit of greenery leading to a grille which opens on to a small "rio" shades the palace garden *(left)*—one of the few gardens of Venice—linked to the palace itself by a footbridge spanning another "rio," whose footbridge *(above foreground)* is garlanded with foliage. The high façade with its rough coating of plaster has arched windows surmounted by stone pediments. In the background, the three bays fronted by a balcony as well as the ones surmounting them are those of the two large "portego" on the first and second floors. The palace dates from the close of the sixteenth century.

The garden was subsequently laid out on the site formerly occupied by the San Cassiano Theater, famous for having been the first theater where the public was admitted to the performance of an opera—no doubt a work by Monteverdi.

A fine lacework of Pompeian arabesques decorates the vault of one of the salons on the first floor, redecorated at the beginning of the nineteenth century under the leadership of Borsato. The figures, the birds, the antique-style tripods, the cassolettes, the draperies, the architectural motifs, linked by acanthus leaves, are divided with a perfect knowledge of balance. The whole composition is painted with delightful freedom.

The marmoreal effect of the bust of *The Beautiful Helen* sculptured by Antonio Canova illuminates the red salon *(below)*. Actually it is a portrait of Countess Isabella Teotochi-Albrizzi, ancestor of the present owners of the palace, named by Byron "the Madame de Staël of Venice." Her salon was famous in the early nineteenth century. The room has preserved its splendid red damask dating from the early eighteenth century when the stucco overdoors were also executed—a glimpse of one of them is caught between the volutes of the chandelier of Venetian glass. The console and the mirror above of gilt wood are among the finest productions of Venetian eighteenth-century craftsmen.

A swarm of cherubs, assisted by graceful adolescent figures of boys and girls, supports the stucco draperies which form the ceiling of the ballroom. We find them again above the doors supporting medallions in the midst of palm trees and cornucopias. This prodigious decoration, executed in 1712, is entirely white and gold. The Venetian furnishings, also in gilt, date from the eighteenth century. On the console stands a candelabrum, executed from a model by Canova, framed by two groups of Meissen porcelain. The portrait above, attributed to Pietro Longhi, represents a member of the Albrizzi family. The floor, paved with irregular fragments of marble mosaic known as "terrazzo," is partly covered by an eighteenth-century Spanish carpet of various fabrics.

Emerging from a network of palm trees, garlands and volutes, figurines of women and children, in the "portego" of the first floor *(below)*, surmount the doors and paintings, and flutter to the ceiling around three large medallions painted by Pelligrini. The large compositions framed in the stucco of the walls are by Sebastiano Mazzoni, Antonio Zanchi, Pietro Liberi and Pacceco di Rosa. The entire decoration with its heavy touch of the Baroque dates from 1670. The furniture, like the chandeliers and the brackets of Murano glass, dates from the eighteenth century. The open-back sofas are characteristic of the Venetian production of this period. The Spanish carpets are similar to those of the ballroom *(preceding double page)*.

The tarnished mirrors of the music salon *(right)* reflect a sumptuous decoration of Pompeian arabesques, garlands and trophies modeled in white stucco against a gold background. In a niche near the window a *Dancing Mercury* brandishes his caduceus. The room dates in its present state from the 1770s and has preserved its important original Venetian furnishings, including here a sumptuously carved wood-gilt chair.

# *Palazzo Frigimelica-Selvatico*

Padua

The cour d'honneur of the palace—seen here through the entrance grille of the grand salon—is bordered on three of its sides by an arcaded gallery with embossed decoration. On the noble story shallow niches adorned with shells continued the arched bays. This fine design, which is notable for its restraint, dates from the second half of the seventeenth century. In fact, it was from 1660 to 1683 that the palace, whose origin dates from the close of the fourteenth century, acquired its present aspect. The last attic story, however, was added at the end of the eighteenth century and for this reason, the statues by Muttoni, placed above the noble story, are no longer silhouetted against the sky, as was originally the case.

Two buxom young women in rustic dress, the work of the sculptor Pietro Danieletti, command the pillars of the grille placed at the far end of the garden. Beyond we see an architectural decoration arranged in 1778-1779. This grille, executed by the ironworker Giacomo Solda in 1779, is adorned by a pediment entirely of rocaille volutes surmounted by a county crown.

The grand salon on the first floor, which is reached by means of a door at the far end on the left, opening on to the grand staircase, dates for the most part from the work executed at the close of the eighteenth century. It was during this period that the room was heightened by the construction of an attic story leading to the arrangement of a vault, decorated with frescoed medallions by Antonio Buttafogo in 1777. On the other hand, the niches, the framework of the doors and windows, with their handsome Baroque pediments inlaid with marble of various colors, seem to date from the second half of the seventeenth century. The polished walnut furniture is eighteenth-century Venetian.

Magnificently designed, the straight staircase rises in three successive landings *(right)* to the grand salon on the first story *(below)*. The base is framed by Doric and Ionic columns followed by pilasters until finally the stairs reach a niche which completes the perspective. The columns are both fluted and annuleted—in the case of the Doric columns the rings even acquire the aspect of helical volutes. The borders, moreover, are designed in the least classical manner and treated with much Baroque fantasy. The Jupiterean eagle placed on the keystone of the arcade was sculptured by Muttoni in 1678, while the two female figures carrying cornucopias, dated 1683, are the work of Antonio Maggi.

# *Villa Valmarana dei Nani*

Vicenza

There is a poetic legend attached to the strange figures of midgets arranged on the walls of the garden *(above)* who gave their name to the villa Valmarana "dei Nani." A young girl belonging to the Valmarana family had the misfortune of being born a dwarf. In order to hide her infirmity her father had raised her in the villa, in the utmost isolation, with only a handful of servants, who were also dwarfs. The girl grew up and one day from her window saw a handsome rider galloping through the countryside. Suddenly realizing her abnormality, she killed herself. On discovering her body the servants were petrified with sorrow, and it is these figures whom we see portrayed on the garden wall.

Construction of the villa proper was undertaken in 1669 from the design by Antonio Muttoni. It was his son Francesco who in the eighteenth century built the "foresteria" or guesthouse close by the villa and adorned with a handsome portico *(left)* fronted by a terrace paved with pebbles.

Just as the high priest Calchas is about to sacrifice Iphigenia *(following double page)*, the victim who willingly offers her throat to the knife, Artemis (represented on the ceiling of the room not shown here) substitutes a doe, which we discover on the left on a cushion of clouds. On the far right, Agamemnon, terrified, hides his face in his cloak. The fresco, executed in 1757 by Gianbattista Tiepolo, adorns one of the walls of the great central "portego" of the villa. Bathed in a clear silvery light, the work, by its very theatrical character, is an example of a kind of genius of decorative effect. The entire composition, centered on the languidly sinuous silhouette of Iphigenia, is superbly framed by the *trompe-l'œil* architectural decoration, executed by Mengozzi Colonna.

On her knees a Chinese woman is piously offering a goddess, hieratically stylized beneath a parasol, a gift of fruit *(left)*. This is the delightful fresco that Giandomenico Tiepolo, the great painter's son, executed to decorate the "stanza cinese" or Chinese Room of the "foresteria." Entirely suitable to the taste for "chinoiserie" which had invaded Europe as early as the end of the seventeenth century, the painting makes no claim to exactitude in its search for exotism. Only the porcelain bottle standing at the foot of the altar is authentically Far Eastern. But the hirsute figure with a heavy mustache and the woman garbed in all her finery, seen in the foreground, are treated with delightful fantasy and humor.

What strikes us at once in the "stanza della villeggiatura," *(above)* likewise situated in the "foresteria," is the extraordinary neo-Gothic decoration imagined by Mengozzi Colonna. It was quite exceptional at the time it was executed (1757), other than in England, where Horace Walpole had launched the fashion some years earlier. In an offhand manner, however, the painter placed in this decoration busts and statues, also in *trompe-l'oeil,* in the most classic taste. The countryside painted by Giandomenico Tiepolo in the central panel represents a summer promenade; on the other walls are spring and winter promenades. These contemporary scenes are treated with a familiar verve which call to mind Goya's tapestry designs.

# *Villa Pisani*

Palace rather than villa, owing to its great dimensions, the edifice *(above)* is surprising for the purity of its design and the restraint of its decoration, considering the date of its construction—1735—at the height of the Rococo period. The Palladian tradition is evident in the skillful arrangement of its vertical volume—a central main building surmounted by a pediment connected by much lower wings to terminal pavilions also surmounted by pediments. Erected on an embossed substructure, Ionic pilasters heighten the composition which is animated by the statues above the roof. Opposite this façade, at the far end of the flowerbed, the stables *(right and following double page)* close the perspective. More lively in design, with their central portico, their turrets and their rounded wings, they were executed in 1735 from the design by the architect Girolamo Frigimelica, who died in 1732. The villa, on the other hand, is the work of Maria Preti. The large artificial lake which links the two buildings was created at the close of the nineteenth century.

On the ballroom ceiling the figure of Fame trumpets the news, Genius brandishes palm leaves and crowns, people in the distance with strange feathers in their hair cry out in celebration of the triumph of the House of Pisani, while Discord and Envy flee in fright. Venice, topped by her towers, witnesses the spectacle wearing a sumptuous robe draped in the most skillful manner. Tiepolo with his sense of dazzling decoration has succeeded in grouping the numerous figures in the composition and who hover in a splendidly luminous sky. This ceiling was the last work which the artist executed in 1761-1762 in Italy before his departure for Spain, where Charles III had summoned him to decorate the Royal Palace at Madrid. The *trompe-l'oeil* architecture which adorns the walls is the work of his assistant Mengozzi Colonna; the chandelier and balcony are by Visconti.

# *Palazzo Treves de' Bonfilii* Venice

Set in one of the finest urban landscapes in the world, at the entrance to the Grand Canal and at the corner of the San Moisè canal, the palace *(left)* is the result of a joining of the seventeenth-century Palazzo Barozzi, whose façade facing the San Moisè canal is attributed both to Bartolomeo Manopola and Baldasarre Longhena, and of a house close by, the Casa Zucchelli. The work, carried out in 1828, was directed by the architect Meduna who had previously rebuilt the Venice Theater. The Casa Zucchelli was raised a story to attain the height of the present palace, and the apartments were enlarged and reshaped to form a homogeneous ensemble.

The interior decoration of the palace was entrusted to Borsato, who was responsible for the delightful Pompeian decoration of the villa at Stra and of the second floor of the Palazzo Albrizzi. He also probably designed the furniture. In the large "portego," the console and the mirror above it are still in the strictly neo-classic taste, but the divan, although pure in design, with its cushion back and its cushions, reflects the search for comfort so eagerly sought in the second half of the nineteenth century. The two paintings of the Venetian Romantic School represent the Piazza of St. Mark and the Seine seen from the Pont-Neuf.

The colossal statues of Hector and Ajax are the last works executed by Antonio Canova shortly before his death in 1822. The two heroes face each other before the combat celebrated by Homer in Book VII of the *Iliad,* "like flesh-eating lions, or like wild boars, whose strength is not to be despised." Their "ideal" beauty conforms to the rules of neo-classicism of which Canova was among the most relentless promoters. Considered in the early nineteenth century the greatest sculptor of his period and one of the greatest of all times, the artist aroused the enthusiasm of Stendhal, who wrote: "Canova had the courage not to copy the Greeks and to invent a beauty as the Greeks had done." The statues were placed in the palace in 1828 in a room specially laid out for them.

# *Palazzo Emo Capodilista*

The palace staircase, added in the eighteenth century to the original thirteenth-century fortress, was designed by the architect Novello, who later worked at the Royal Palace in Madrid. The landing on the first floor, adorned with massive Corinthian pilasters, is crowned, above a console cornice, by a cupola on pendentives in whose center is an oculus which provides this handsome architectural feature with a soft glow of light. The very simple stucco decoration emphasizes the purity of the design.

The death of Lucrezia, among the favorite themes of Venetian eighteenth-century painters, is the subject of one of the frescoes which decorate the grand "portego" of the palace *(above)*, the work of Antonio Buttafogo executed in the second half of the eighteenth century. The sumptuous stucco decoration on the walls is lavishly ornate. The glasswork of the doors, consisting of geometrically arranged panes set in a network of lead, is similar in design to the windows of numerous palaces in the region of Venice and Padua.

The *trompe-l'oeil* decoration of one of the salons *(right)*, the work of Tiepolo's pupil, Francesco Zugno, represents huge bays opening on to the architectural landscapes. The child seated on the balustrade, held in the arms of an elegantly attired nanny, is reaching out to his parents, members of the Capodilista family, to whom the palace belonged when these frescoes were executed about 1770-1780. The sofa and the chairs with their subtly undulating lines are Venetian and also date from the eighteenth century.

MDLXXX
MARCVS·ANTONIVS·BARBARVS·PROCVRATOR·FRANC·FILIVS

# *Villa Barbaro*

Maser

From the gardens adorned with statues which, facing the villa, descend as far as the entrance portal *(left and above)*, we catch a glimpse of the Tempietto, which in fact is a chapel erected, like the villa itself, about 1560 by Palladio at the request of Marcantonio Barbaro. The edifice consists of a central circular room inscribed in a square and topped by a cupola surmounted by a lantern turret. It is linked to the portico with its Corinthian columns by two small campaniles; the portico is very similar to that of the temple of Castor and Pollux at Rome, as represented by Palladio in *I Quattro Libri dell'Architettura*. The elegant and noble mass of the Tempietto looms proudly over the land and dominates the vast stretches of the countryside.

The center of the villa *(cf. following double page and the plan on page 97)* consists of the "casa padronale," designed for the owners, which is framed by two arcaded wings terminating in two pavilions whose high pediments are adorned with sundials. The pavilions contain the dovecotes, the stables and various outbuildings, including, according to Palladio himself, "the places where wine is made." The architect was able to combine in a lavish architectural composition the sumptuousness necessary to a patrician dwelling and the requirements of a country residence. The "casa padronale," projecting to a marked degree from the entrance façade, is decorated with a colossal order of Ionic columns, supported by a pediment sculptured with coats-of-arms and figures. The garden gently descends to the road and is continued, beyond the fountain seen in the foreground, by an avenue lined with trees.

The room in the form of a cross which occupies the center of the main building projecting from the entrance façade *(right and plan)* is devoted to Harmony and Music, so highly esteemed at Venice, whose singers and performers were famous throughout Europe. On two arms of the cross, eight majestic female figures (two of whom are seen here) hold various instruments, including a flute, an oboe, a tambourine and a lute. On the other arms, huge bays open on to rustic landscapes. The *trompe-l'oeil* decoration includes doors where children and pages appear. The room was originally even more charming when a pergola with trellis providing a view of the sky was painted on the vaults, as attested by the description given by Redolfi in his biography of Veronese.

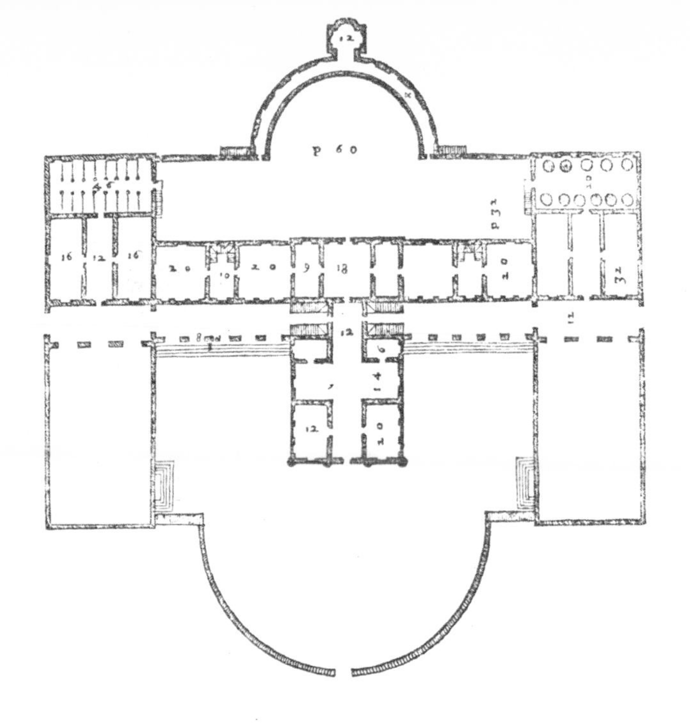

The ceiling in the Olympus Room, situated in the center of the façade overlooking the garden, is decorated with frescoes by Veronese. The central section depicts Universal Harmony who is shown slaying a dragon. Surrounding him are the planets, represented by the gods and goddesses of antiquity. We recognize Mercury and his caduceus; Diana, goddess of the Moon, with her dogs; Saturn and Jupiter. The Four Elements, symbolized by Cybele (visible on the right), Neptune, Juno and Vulcan, occupy those sections left free by the octagonal frame which contains the composition. Skillful, elaborate and suitable to the humanistic spirit of the Renaissance, the composition was suggested to Veronese, who executed these frescoes about 1561, by the Barbaro brothers, learned and cultured men to whom the villa belonged. Beneath the splendid vault, on the *trompe-l'oeil* balcony which dominates the room, the painter represented the wife of Marcantonio Barbaro with her old nurse and one of her sons, who is looking at a parrot. From one of the doors of the Olympus Room we glimpse the series of rooms facing the garden and notice a false door, where someone in hunting dress is standing. According to tradition, the figure is none other than Veronese.

Painted freely and in a light style recalling watercolor technique, one of the landscapes which decorate the Room of Bacchus *(below)* shows an imaginary villa at the far end of a long avenue bordered by trees with carriages and horsemen. Throughout the house we come upon these rustic scenes, "views" adorned with villas or ruins which create a "hole" in the walls and make each room a belvedere opening wide to the Venetian landscape.

Behind the villa, closing the perspective of the "giardino segreto," stands the nympheum *(opposite)* framing a sheet of water. Built in the form of a semicircle and crowned by a pediment, it leads to a shady grotto. Its rich decoration of statues, garlands, rinceaux and trophies is the work of the sculptor Alessandro Vittoria.

CALLE
DONA

# *Palazzo Donà dalle Rose*

The first stone of the Pallazo Donà dalle Rose was laid on March 24, 1610, on the eve of the Feast of the Annunciation, which tradition held to be the day when Venice had magically risen from the water. One of its façades *(left)* faces a "rio"; the other, almost similar, stands on the Fondamente Nuove, opposite the lagoon seen in the distance. Very simple in design and bearing a pink coating of plaster, it is enlivened by the central portal surmounted by three Palladian windows and a balcony. The palace was built for the doge Leonardo Donà dalle Rose, whose portrait *(above)* by an unknown painter reveals his energetic character. Indeed, he proved of utmost courage during the struggle between Venice and the Papacy which occurred during his reign. The doge was well assisted in his trial by Fra Paolo Sarpi who is said to have designed the palace.

A large model of a seventeenth-century ship *(opposite)* is exhibited in the "portego" on the first floor. This grand gallery, typical of Venetian villas and palaces, spans the edifice and has windows at both ends. The "portego" recalls the maritime exploits of various members of the Donà family, whose portraits adorn its walls in stucco frames which were made at the close of the eighteenth century.

The two superbly wrought lanterns dominating the entrance vestibule on the ground floor of the palace *(above)* were once features of the family galleys which had fought at the battle of Lepanto. The marble slabs of the floor, the panelling which covers the lower section of the walls—adorned above with eighteenth-century stucco—glisten in light streaming from the door which opens on to the lagoon. The scalloped benches with high backs adorned with coats-of-arms are found in most of the great patrician dwellings in Venice.

One of the salons on the first floor is covered with gilt-toned damask *(right)* which forms a warm and delicate harmony with the green, yellow, brown and white stucco door-frames. A portrait of the doge Leonardo Donà has been inserted in the space over the door. Above the eighteenth-century Venetian console with its ship models is a seventeenth-century map showing one of the territories of the ancient Republic of Venice.

Vicenza

# *Villa Rotonda*

Referring to the Villa Rotonda, Goethe in his *Journey to Italy* wrote: "Never perhaps has architecture achieved such a degree of magnificence. The staircase and the porticoes occupy a space quite superior to the villa itself. In fact, each of its four façades could form the magnificent entrance to a temple."

Construction of the villa was undertaken about 1550-1551 from the design by Palladio and it was still unfinished in 1580 when the architect died. The final work was entrusted to Vicenzo Scamozzi. Considered Palladio's masterpiece, the villa exercised great influence on architecture and was imitated by Scamozzi himself at the Rocca Pisana. In England alone there are four versions of the original dating from the eighteenth century during the great vogue of Palladianism: Chiswick, Mereworth, Foot's Cray and Nuttal Temple (the last two have since been razed).

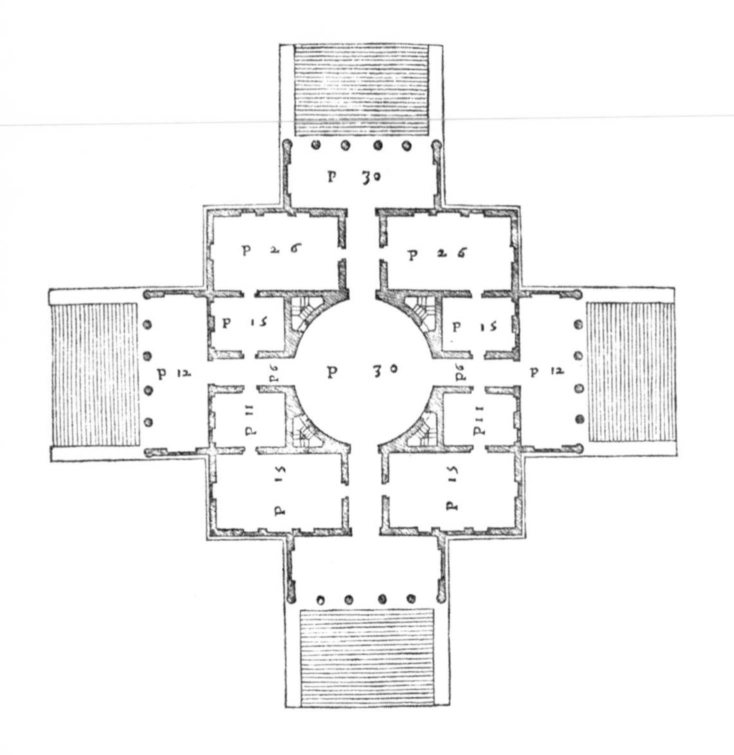


The villa has four identical porticoes on its four sides *(cf. plan opposite)*; the apartments are symmetrically arranged around a central rotunda *(below and right)* which occupies the entire height of the edifice. The room is crowned by a cupola whose center contains an oculus. Four vaulted passages link it with the four entrance portals, and a balcony runs above the first floor. The stucco work of the cupola, executed before 1591, is attributed to Agostino Rubini, nephew of the great sculptor Alessandro Vittoria. The frescoes between the stucco work were painted by Alessandro Maganza from 1599 to 1609. In the early eighteenth century Louis Dorigny, who spent most of his life in Italy, painted the *trompe-l'oeil* architectural decoration and the large Baroque figures which cover the walls of the room beneath the balcony.

# *Lombardy and Liguria*

*Lombardy, the most fertile region of Italy, is bounded on the north by the Alps, on the south by the Po, on the west by Piedmont and on the east by the Mincio River. The vital core of the province is Milan. It was around this city that there arose in the twelfth century the powerful state ruled by the Visconti and later by the Sforza. The stake of struggles with many vicissitudes between the Valois and the Hapsburgs, the Milanese, which had been incorporated with the domains of the house of Austria in 1524, was to remain Spanish until 1713, Austrian from 1713 to 1797. The capital of the Cisalpine Republic, which became the Kingdom of Naples in 1804, Milan followed the destinies of the Napoleonic Empire. In 1815 Lombardy fell under the yoke of Austria, but in 1859 its annexation to Piedmont marked the first step toward Italian unity.*

*Hemmed in between the sea and the Apennines, Liguria, annexed to the French Empire from 1805 to 1814, had been incorporated with Piedmont as early as the Congress of Vienna. Indeed the proud Genoese oligarchy had been unable to prevent the precipitation of a political decadence which the Venetians, like the Turks, had provoked since the fourteenth century. A banking metropolis and an important maritime arsenal, Genoa nevertheless remained the capital of a commercial republic, whose proud palaces still recall the grandeur of its past.*

## Genoa *Palazzo Pallavicini*

The origin of the Pallavicini family dates from Oberto, born in 960, whose descendants, the "Obertenghi," gave birth to some of the most powerful princely houses of Europe, notably the House of Este, the dukes of Brunswick, the Marquis Malaspina, the Marquis of Massa and the Marquis Pallavicini. The Pallavicini House itself was divided into several branches, including the Pallavicini of Parma, Genoa, England (it died out in 1648) and Hungary. The Genoese branch achieved leading importance in the Republic, to whom it gave three doges, fifty-two senators and numerous diplomats.

The Palazzo Pallavicini was built from 1565 to 1575 by the architect Francesco Casella for Marquis Interiano. It then passed into the hands of the marquises Centurione and the marquises Vivaldi-Pasqua. In 1836 it was acquired by the great-grandfather of the present owner, Marquis Domenico Pallavicini, who had the interior decoration modified by the architect Pittaluga between 1844 and 1852. The palace, which contains an important collection of paintings, furniture and porcelain, is now the property of Marquis Ludovico Pallavicini.

## Genoa *Palazzo Doria Principe*

Born in 1466 into one of the oldest and most important Genoese families, Andrea Doria, after a particularly eventful career, proved himself among the greatest admirals of all time. When he was only a boy, his widowed mother entrusted him to one of her husband's relatives, Niccolò Doria, who took charge of his education. Andrea entered the papal guard of Innocent VIII, of which Niccolò was captain, then after the Pope's death, the service of Federigo of Urbino. He then turned to Alfonso II of Aragon, king of Naples, who entrusted him with the command of an expedition against Ludovico il Moro, Duke of Milan.

After Alfonso had been driven from Naples by Charles VII, Andrea became a member of the Order of Saint John of Jerusalem and made a journey to the Holy Land, returning in 1495. But Ferdinand II of Aragon, son of Alfonso, recaptured Naples. Andrea sided with the French and together with Giovanni della Rovere distinguished himself by defending the Rocca Guglielma. He went to Milan to serve Ludovico il Moro, then to Genoa from where in 1503 he subjected rebellious Corsica and kept it under the rule of the Republic. In 1513 he received command of the Genoese fleet and in 1519 won a great naval victory against the Turkish corsairs off Pianosa. Thanks to naval spoils he was able to form a personal fleet of twelve galleys, but he soon found himself forced to leave Genoa, where the Fregosi party, of which he was a member, was destroyed by the Adorini. He then offered his services to Francis I who named him general of the French galleys. He destroyed the Imperial fleet which was wreaking havoc along the Provençal coasts, liberated Marseilles which was besieged by the Connétable de Bourbon and, after the disaster of Pavia, received the remaining French forces, rallied by the Duke of Albany.

During Francis I's captivity at Madrid, he refused the offers of Charles V and became general of Clement VII's papal galleys. But after Francis I's captivity had ended, the French monarch named him general of the galleys of the Levant. Genoa was then in the hands of the Imperials (troops of the Holy Roman emperor) and Andrea in his desire "to combat Genoa for the benefit of Genoa herself," besieged the city, seized it in 1527 and named Teodoro Trivulzio governor for France.

Andrea Doria married Peretta Usodimare, granddaughter of Innocent VIII and the widow of Alfonso del Carretto. He was then at the height of his career. Genoa named him "father and liberator" of the country, offered him a palace in the Piazza San Matteo and erected a statue in his honor. In 1528 he promulgated a new constitution which appeared rather liberal, but all the important posts were actually held by men who had been devoted to him.

A new turning point in his career was marked by an expedition in Sardinia directed against the enemies of France. After a series of brilliant victories—notably the one in which his nephew, Filippo Doria, in the Gulf of Salerno, challenged the Spanish squadron commanded by Moncade, who perished in the combat—Andrea Doria, believing himself to be poorly rewarded by Francis I and solicited by his Spanish prisoners, went over to Charles V, who gave him the princeship of Melfi in 1531. In 1529 he put to flight the French squadron commanded by Barbezieux, who had sailed to assist Odet de Foix Lautrec's attack on Naples, thus definitely destroying French hopes in Italy. He then left to combat the Turks: he captured Coron and Patras in Greece, forcing Solyman II to relax his hold on Austria and Hungary. In 1535 Doria commanded the expedition against Tunis. The following year he participated in the one against Provence; he seized Toulon but was stopped before Marseilles. During the meeting arranged by Pope Paul III between Charles V and Francis I, he found his old master again.

*Giuseppe Verdi*

*The Battle of Lepanto*

"The king," related Pierre de Bourdeilles de Brantôme, "went to the emperor's galley, which was the flagship of Andrea Doria; the emperor begged the king to see him for the love of him and offered him a fine meal; and this the king gladly did, asking him how he was with no mention of the past."

In 1547 his power over Genoa was

almost destroyed by the plot hatched by Giovanni Luigi Fieschi, the famous Fieschi conspiracy which subsequently inspired Schiller to write his drama, *Fiesco or the Genoese Conspiracy*. The conspiracy failed because Fieschi, on his way to his galley, fell into the sea and, weighed down by his armor, drowned. His partisans fled and those who remained were pitilessly executed. Andrea Doria's rancor was tenacious. Eight years later when he succeeded in capturing Ottoboni Fieschi, Giovanni Luigi's brother, he had him sewed in a sack and drowned in the gulf.

The extraordinary thing is that in the midst of all this tremendous activity, Andrea, according to his biographer Carlo Sigonio, still found time "to hear Mass every day and then recite the Virgin's prayer and the Seven Psalms of Penitence." In 1560 he died piously at the age of ninety-four.

The Palazzo Doria Principe (Principe owing to the title Prince of Melfi granted to Andrea Doria by Charles V) was begun in 1521 and finished in 1529. Charles V was received here with great pomp and in 1533 magnificent fêtes were given in his honor. In his will Andrea Doria left the major part of his fortune, including the principality of Melfi, to the son of his wife's first marriage, Marcantonio del Carretto, whom he had adopted. He bequeathed the Palazzo Doria together with his galleys to his grand nephew, Giannadrea Doria, who added the west wing and the lateral loggias, and also made changes in the decoration. Another nephew named Pagano received the counties of Torriglia and Loano which had been seized from the Fieschi.

The palace has since remained the possession of Giannandrea Doria's descendants. It was here that Napoleon, Josephine and his court resided from June 30 to July 6, 1805, after his coronation at Milan. The Ligurian Republic —which during his stay requested its annexation by France—offered the Emperor a sumptuous nautical fête: rafts were converted into floating islands, completely covered with shrubbery and flowers, and musicians in Chinese costumes serenaded the French sovereigns who sailed in a boat decorated as a temple of Neptune.

In 1877 Verdi rented a suite in the palace where he spent a few winter months until 1898. On this occasion his wife, the former cantatrice Giuseppina Strepponi, wrote to the publisher Giulio Ricordi, "This will certainly be the last moving out of this kind . . . the last, the last will be a moving out between four planks . . . and then it will be eternal rest." It was here during the winter of 1884-1885, after a long silence, that Verdi composed the major parts of *Otello*. In this connection, on December 9, 1884 (he was then seventy-one years of age), he wrote to his librettist Boïeto, "This appears impossible and yet it is true! I am busy writing! I am writing . . . because I am writing, with no goal, no preoccupations, no thought of what will follow, and even with a well decided aversion to what will follow."

During World War II the palace suffered from bombardments and has not been wholly restored. It is today the property of Donna Orietta and Don Frank Doria Pamphili Pogson.

## Genoa *Palazzo Durazzo-Pallavicini*

*The Palazzo Durazzo-Pallavicini*

In spite of its name, the Palazzo Durazzo-Pallavicini is not the work of the Durazzo but of the Balbi. In fact, it was Giovanni Agostino Balbi who in 1618 ordered it to be built from the design by Bartolomeo Bianco.

The palace soon passed into the hands of the Durazzo, an ancient family originally from Albania, who, fleeing from the Turks, settled at Genoa in 1388 and acquired Genoese citizenship the following year. On the occasion of the constitution of 1528 established by Andrea Doria which reserved political power to a limited number of families grouped into "alberghi," the Durazzo belonged to the "albergo Grimaldi." Having amassed a considerable fortune, they gave the Church two cardinals and the Republic nine doges. Piero Durazzo, doge from 1685 to 1687, raised the city from its ruins after the bombardment ordered by Louis XIV. Marcellino, whose rule as doge lasted from 1767 to 1769, ceded Corsica to France.

From 1778 to 1780 the palace underwent transformations executed from the design of the architect Andrea Tagliafichi; at that time the marquis even thought of decorating the façade in a more sumptuous manner, but the project was not carried out.

The last marquis of the Durazzo family, Giacomo Filippo, who died in 1921, was authorized by a royal decree of August 20, 1873, to add to his name that of his mother, Teresa Pallavicini. His widow, *née* Princess Matilda Giustiniani, has lovingly preserved this splendid residence, with its fine collection of paintings, furniture and art objects, and its superb library rich in illuminated manuscripts and incunabula.

## Mantua *Palazzo del Tè*

"The greatest pain I could suffer would be to displease Your Excellency," wrote Giulio Romano to Federigo, Marquis of Mantua, on August 31, 1528. "My greatest joy is to retain your favor and if Your Grace so desires, I beg him to lock me up in this salon until it is finished." In 1524, the Marquis of Mantua had received the artist who had been driven from Rome after a scandal (he had supplied Marcantonio Raimondi with the drawings for the engravings illustrating Aretino's *Luxurious Sonnets*) and at once commissioned him to draw up the plans of a small palace outside the city gates, on land partly occupied by the celebrated Gonzaga stud farms. The architectural work was rapidly executed, but the interior decoration was not finished until 1535, resulting in recriminations by the marquis and protests by Giulio Romano who, in spite of the help of several assistants, was exhausted by this huge undertaking.

When ordering this palace, Federigo certainly had in mind a more pleasant atmosphere than the ducal palace as a setting for his love affair with the beautiful and imperious Isabella Boschetti. Their liaison probably began about 1520 and at that time Isabella was already a member of the young marquis' suite during a trip to Venice. She was married as a matter of form to Francesco Calvisano of the youngest branch of the House of Gonzaga and soon reigned officially and completely in the heart of her lover. Their liaison much displeased the old marquise, Isabella d'Este, mother of Federigo. Ambitious and vindictive, Isabella Boschetti demanded and obtained every respect due a titled sovereign. A contemporary described "the marquis' mistress proudly crossing the city on horseback, followed by all the gentilshommes who normally accompanied the old marquise. For her entire escort the latter had merely one or two old men."

La Boschetti, who had presented three children to Federigo, sought to use every means to prevent his marriage. Her arrogance led to a conspiracy to eliminate her, but it was discovered and failed. She attempted to attribute the responsibility to the Marquise of Montferrat, mother of the duke's fiancée. In 1531, the duke finally married the sister of this fiancée, who had died in the meantime—yet in no way did he modify his attitude toward his mistress.

In 1530, the Palazzo del Tè was the scene of the splendid reception offered to Charles V by Federigo who on the occasion of the sovereign's visit was made duke.

At the close of the sixteenth century, Agnès de Argotta, daughter of a Cordovan gentleman and mistress of Duke Vincenzo I, a woman of culture and intelligence, held a brilliant court at the palace, surrounding herself with scholars and scientists. In 1630, the splendid apartments were defaced during the sack of Mantua. After the Gonzaga dynasty had come to an end in 1708, the Palazzo del Tè was left in a pitiful state. Charles de Brosses visited it in 1739 and wrote: "The place does not contain the slightest piece of furniture and no one lives here; it remains abandoned and completely open, like a barn." Then, speaking of *The Fall of the Titans* which adorned one of the rooms, he added: "This work which is the artist's triumph is well worthy of a full description and in the excess of my flow of speech I would not care to do so if it had not already been done by Félibien, where you can see it. But what would this great orator of painting say if he knew that this incomparable salon was finally used as a guardroom for a handful of miserable German soldiers who, by the most Teutonic of all barbaric means, have written their names on and done a thousand other cruelties to this painting?"

Henceforth the fate of the Palazzo del Tè was linked with that of the palace of Mantua. After belonging to Austria, then to France, then again to Austria in 1815, it was acquired in 1866 by the Crown of Italy. Restored, it is now the property of the city of Mantua.

## Mantua *Reggia*

*So rich your line of descendants will one day finally lead*
*To that friend of the arts,*
*Full of grace and charm,*
*Wisdom and pure habits, Isabella.*

Thus the prophetess Melissa in *Orlando Furioso* offers Bradamante, the mythical founder of the House of Este, the portrait of Isabella d'Este, Marquise of Mantua. Ariosto, who since 1503 had been in the service of Cardinal Hippolyte d'Este, brother of Isabella, met the latter for the first time in 1507 and worshipped her.

Isabella d'Este's letters, which were numerous, her art collections (now dispersed), the setting in which she lived after her widowhood and still visible at Reggia, all help to recreate a lively personage. We can easily imagine her engaged in poetry, music and the arts as well as in politics during the troubled period when the small court at Mantua had to navigate cautiously, since it was constantly being tossed between the Pope and his son, Cesare Borgia, the German emperor and the king of France.

The fortunes of the Gonzagas had begun with Luigi Gonzaga who became lord of Mantua in 1328 after driving out the Bonacolsi.

The family's ascendancy continued to the fifteenth century and in 1433 the emperor granted Gianfrancesco II the title of marquis. His son Ludovico had been raised by Vittorino da Feltre in her celebrated "casa giocosa" where boys and girls of every rank, chosen for their intelligence, received a fine education, including not only Platonic theories but those of Christian morality, physical exercise and lessons in contemporary courtly manners. It was Ludovico who summoned Alberti and Mantegna to Mantua, commissioning the latter to decorate the Camera degli Sposi with his splendid frescoes. Politian's *Orfeo,* the ancestor of Italian opera, was given before Ludovico's court in 1470. The reign of his successor Federigo I was short (1478-1484). Federigo's son, Francesco, was only eighteen when he ascended the throne

Ariosto *by Titian*

and his wife Isabella d'Este found herself at the head of one of the most brilliant courts of Italy.

Her first concern was to install a private apartment, including its famous "studiolo." The decoration of this apartment today no longer occupies its initial site in the Castello San Giorgio, for in 1523, after her widowhood, she had it transported, remounted and completed in the "Corte Vecchia," another section of the palace. In 1502 Isabella wrote: "We would like for our small cabinet historical subjects painted by the best Italian artists." By 1497 Mantegna had executed for the "studiolo" *Parnassus* and *Minerva Expelling the Vices and Virtues*, Perugino a *Combat of Chastity and Voluptuousness*, Lorenzo Costa *The Court of the Muses of Isabella d'Este*. Each time the marquise had given the painters a precise program which very probably had been established by the classical scholars of her court. In regard to this she wrote to Perugino: "The poetical subject we wish to be treated by you is the conflict between Purity and Voluptuousness, represented in the struggle of Pallas and Diana against Venus and Love. . . ." Two pages of detailed instructions followed. In 1532, when she changed her apartment, she had the "studiolo" decoration completed by Correggio's *Triumph of Virtue* and *Man a Slave of the Vices*, now in the Louvre.

The Virgin of Victory *by Mantegna*

Her curiosity extended to statues, art objects and books. In the inventory made after her death there were found antique works, including a bust of Faustina which had belonged to Mantegna and is among the rare pieces to have remained at the Reggia, bronzes by Riccio, medals and books by the famous Venetian printer Aldus Manutius, which he personally offered to Isabella. "You will prove benevolent to all these scholarly and virtuous persons," he wrote to her, "you who are distinguished for your great culture and high morality. This will increase my devotion on your behalf. I would like to express this feeling by offering you a few proofs of my knowledge."

Isabella's means of procuring the objects she coveted were not always beyond reproach. For example, she had seen at the home of her sister-in-law and intimate friend, Elizabeth, Duchess of Urbino, a *Sleeping Cupid* by the young Michelangelo (which, unfortunately, is now lost). When Cesare Borgia captured Urbino in 1502 he seized all the works of art in the palace. Isabella used every means of gaining possession of the *Cupid* and, thanks to the intervention of Cardinal d'Este, Cesare finally granted her wish. Before taking such steps she had, it is true, requested authorization from her sister-in-law. But when the Duke and Duchess of Urbino regained their possessions and demanded that Michelangelo's sculpture be returned to them, they were met with furious opposition which Isabella tried to justify by questionable means. She finally kept her *Cupid*.

Although less attracted to the arts than his wife, Francesco commissioned a *Virgin of Victory* from Mantegna to commemorate the victory of Fornovo; it was placed in the small Church of Victory at Mantua in 1496 (the painting is now in the Louvre). He also commissioned the splendid *Triumphs of Caesar*, now at the Hampton Court. Francesco died in 1519 and was succeeded by Federigo, his nineteen-year-old son. Partly raised at the Roman court of Julius II and partly at the court of France, Federigo had inherited from his mother a love of art and luxury which brought him to the point of extravagance. In 1525 his residence numbered 600 persons and his stud farms, famous throughout Italy, 400 horses. In 1524 he commissioned Giulio Romano to decorate a section of the Reggia and the Castello San Giorgio, adding new apartments there (the Paleologa, the Rustica, the Corte Nuova) and design the Palazzo del Tè. Federigo was also a great lover of painting. Less "literary" than his mother, in 1524 he wrote to Sebastiano del Piombo: "What I want from you are pleasant refreshing paintings to look at." But to decorate his apartments he asked Titian to paint an *Entombment*, now in the Louvre, and a series of the *Twelve Caesars*. He already possessed Titian's *Pilgrims of Emmaus*, originally intended for a church in Venice, as well as *The Virgin with a Rabbit* and the *Portrait of Balthazar Castiglione*, both by Raphael, and a *Pastoral Symphony*, all now in the Louvre. On the occasion of the coronation of Charles V by Pope Clement VII in 1530 at Bologna, he commissioned three paintings from Correggio to be presented to the Emperor. After being included in imperial collections, these works were acquired by Christina of Sweden, then by the Regent and were dispersed during the Revolution. The subjects were *Danaë* (Villa Borghese), *Leda* (Berlin Museum) and *Ion* (Berlin Museum). Splendid fêtes marked the receptions offered to the Emperor in his palace, in March and April 1530, immediately after the coronation. The whole city had been decorated with allegorical triumphal arches designed by Giulio Romano. One of the hunts numbered no less than 5,000 horsemen. Federigo received the title of Duke of Mantua.

On his death in 1540, his brother Ercole Gonzaga became regent in the name of his nephews Francesco II, who died in 1550, and Guglielmo. A wise administrator, he sought above all to pay his brother's debts. Guglielmo commissioned Tintoretto to decorate the "appartamento maggiore" of the palace with a series of huge compositions devoted to the great deeds of the Gonzagas (these are now in the Munich Pinakothek). Vincenzo I, son of Guglielmo, was the patron of Rubens and Monteverdi. The first was court painter at Mantua from 1600 to 1608, and in spite of his frequent absence at Rome, Genoa and in Spain, he executed various paintings of attractive women for the duke's portrait gallery as well as copies from the masters. On Vincenzo's orders he decorated the Jesuit church at Mantua with a *Holy Trinity Adored by Vincenzo of Gonzaga and His Family* (it is now in the Reggia, but in a badly mutilated state), a *Transfiguration* (Nancy Museum) and a *Baptism of Christ* (Antwerp Museum).

In 1590 Monteverdi entered the service of Vincenzo, whose orchestra was famous throughout Italy, first as a mere musician, then as director of the "Sinfonia Ducale." It was to entertain the court that he composed his Second, Third, Fourth and Fifth Books of Madrigals, his *Orfeo* given for the first time in 1607 and his *Arianna* (1608) in addition to numerous religious works. In 1613 he left Mantua for Venice.

The death of Vincenzo I in 1612 marked the beginning of the decline of the Gonzaga dynasty. When his son Francesco died only a few months after him, his second son Ferdinand succeeded him, followed in 1626 by Vincenzo II. During his short reign—he died in 1627—the latter ceded to Charles I of England the chief part of his rich collection of paintings of the House of Gonzaga. After the death of the King of England these works, with the exception of *The Triumphs of Caesar*, were sold by Parliament, and Mazarin acquired a few which he bequeathed to Louis XIV. They are now in the Louvre. The death of Vincenzo II, who left no children, posed the problem of the succession of Mantua. The duke had left his estates to a distant cousin, Charles of Gonzaga, Duke of Nevers, a member of the French branch of this house, who won the support of Richelieu and of Venice, while the Emperor supported the candidature of Cesare of Gonzaga, duke of Guastalla. The Imperials seized Mantua in 1630 and the Reggia as well as the city were sacked. However, Charles gained possession of his estates. He was the father of Louisa Maria of Gonzaga, Queen of Poland, and of Anna of Gonzaga, Princess Palatine, whose funeral oration was given by the noted orator and prelate, Jacques Bossuet. Charles sold a part of Isabella d'Este's library to Victor Emmanuel of Savoy. The works of Mantegna, Perugino and Lorenzo Costa which decorated the "studiolo" were acquired by Richelieu in 1630, then by the king and finally by the Louvre.

Pastoral Symphony *by Giorgione*

The last member of the Gonzaga family died in 1708. His possessions were sold by his heir, the Duke of Lorraine, the great canvases by Tintoretto being acquired by the Elector of Bavaria. His estates were shared between Savoy, which took Montferrat, and Austria, which received the Mantuan domain. Henceforth the Reggia was occupied only rarely. Maria Theresa stayed there during her trips to the Italian states and had certain apartments redecorated.

From 1797 to 1815, Mantua was a part of the Cisalpine Republic, then of the Kingdom of Italy. Certain rooms in the palace were then decorated in the Empire style.

In 1814 one of them was the scene of the birth of Théolinde de Beauharnais, future Countess of Württemberg, daughter of Viceroy Eugène and of Amélie-Auguste of Bavaria, who later fled before the Austrian armies.

In 1815 Austria regained possession of Mantua and in 1866 ceded it to the King of Italy. The palace was rarely inhabited in the nineteenth century and now belongs to the Italian State.

## Bogliaco *Villa Bettoni*

Construction of the Villa Bettoni was undertaken in the early eighteenth century by Gian Domenico Bettoni, born of an old family of the region. In the fourteenth century one of his ancestors, Giacomino, was in the service of Venice and had distinguished himself at the head of the Republic's armies. Zanetto Bettoni had fought alongside Philip II of Spain at the battle of Saint-Quentin. Carlo Bettoni had died in the sixteenth century in the odor of sanctity and had been beatified. As for Gian Domenico, he had cleverly negotiated for the Emperor

*Count Delay Bettoni*

Charles VI the adhesion of the Elector of Bavaria to the "pragmatic sanction." The affair was delicate: the "Leopoldine arrangement" made by Emperor Leopold in 1703 stated that if his elder son, the future Joseph I, died without a male heir (which had in fact happened), the succession would go to his second son Charles, but that in the event the latter also had only daughters, the succession would fall to Joseph's daughters by primogeniture. Charles VI had only one daughter, the future Empress Maria Theresa—and in spite of the "Leopoldine arrangement" which he had sworn to respect—he wanted to assure his states to Maria Theresa and therefore promulgated the "pragmatic sanction." Gian Domenico's mission was to have the Elector of Bavaria, who had married Maria Amalia, daughter of Joseph I, renounce the Hapsburg heritage in favor of Maria Theresa. Although Gian Domenico succeeded in his mission —he was rewarded with the title of Count of the Holy Empire—on the death of Charles VI the promises then given were promptly broken.

It was, however, Gian Antonio Bettoni (1717-1773) who not only brought the greatest titles of glory to his house but also finished the magnificent villa begun by Gian Domenico. Having offered his sword to the service of Maria Theresa, he was destined to lose an eye while fighting the Turks and especially distinguish himself during the Seven Years' War. As field marshal in command of the Imperial cavalry, he avoided a catastrophic retreat during the victory of Frederick II of Prussia at Torgau in 1760. At Lem, Posnania, two years later, during the short reign of Peter III, he succeeded at the head of his regiments in routing the troops led by the Russian general Romanov. At the end of the war he was named General Inspector of the Imperial Cavalry not only in the hereditary states but in Italy as well. He had the elegance to renounce the rich appanages which has been granted him in order not to encumber the exhausted finances of the Empire. It is said that on learning of his death, Maria Theresa could not hold back her tears.

The plans of the Villa Bettoni were made by the architect Adriano Cristofori, and those of the gardens by Amerigo Vicenzo Pierallini. Work was finished about 1760.

Princely guests stayed at the villa on several occasions. On July 23, 1765, the future emperor Joseph II and his suite danced until dawn in the grand salon, then went to fish for "carpione," a form of trout caught in Lake Garda. In 1796 Murat established his headquarters at the Villa Bettoni. In 1806 magnificent fêtes were offered here in honor of Eugène de Beauharnais, Viceroy of Italy, and of his wife Augusta of Bavaria. During the War of Independence in 1866 Garibaldi's troops were quartered in the lemon greenhouses, as is evident by various inscriptions on the walls and also on the statues in the park.

The villa sufferred even more in 1943 when it was occupied by SS troops. The damage was repaired and the villa once again resembles what it was in the eighteenth century, thanks to the effort and vigilant care on the part of countesses Clara and Maria Bettoni Cazzago.

## Montirone *Villa Lechi*

At the Villa Lechi, on June 13, 1805, Countess Lechi, surrounded by her eleven children, greeted Napoleon and his suite, marshals Berthier, Bessières, Mortier, Brune and Moncey, the Master of the Horse Caulaincourt, Bertrand, Savary and Rapp, the Chamberlain Rémusat and others. Only a few days before, the Emperor had been crowned King of Italy at Milan and from Montirone could easily direct the maneuvers taking place at Montichiari. On the evening of his arrival, the gardens and the villa were brilliantly illuminated. The following day he received various delegations and as usual dictated several important letters. One of these, addressed to Eugène de Beauharnais, discussed the organization of the Kingdom of Italy. In another he gave his instructions to Admiral Decrès concerning fleet movements in view of a landing in England. On the morning of June 15 he left the villa for Verona. The porcelain and glass service used during his stay can still be seen at the villa.

At the close of the seventeenth century the domain of Montirone belonged to Francesco Crotta degli Acerbi who, on August 12, 1701, received here Prince Eugene, commander of the Imperial armies, and his staff. On the following September 1 the prince defeated Villeroy at the battle of Chiari. Some years later the domain was acquired by the Lechi brothers—Pietro, Bernardino and the abbot Angelo—who in 1724 received the feudal induction of the bishop of Brescia. It was Count Pietro who made the domain his summer residence. In a clever manner and often "at the risk of his life," states a decree of the Venetian senate, he defended the interests of the Republic at the court of Austria, thus reestablishing the fortune of his family which in the early sixteenth century had to emigrate to Valtrompia.

Soon the seventeenth-century villa which he had found at Montirone appeared insufficient and together with his brothers he decided, in 1735, to undertake the reconstruction while preserving various sections. The design of the new edifice was commissioned from Gian Antonio Turbino, an architect born at Lugano but living at Brescia, where he had built several palaces and redecorated the Palazzo Lechi. Work was begun in 1739 and finished in 1744. The interior decoration was executed by the Milanese painter Giacomo Lecchi, and Carlo Carloni. The chapel was built in 1754, the stables in 1756, and the creation of the gardens extended until about 1760.

On the death of Count Pietro Lechi

in 1764, the villa passed into the hands of his two sons, Faustino and Galeano. Although he preserved the right to reside there, Faustino abandoned the ownership of the dwelling to his brother. The latter, who had a haughty character, perpetuated the tradition of the "tyrants" of Brescia, surrounding himself with a group of villains and leading a princely existence. He collected at Montirone all kinds of weapons and arranged the suites for his numerous guests. His excess and intransigence, however, knew no bounds, and the Republic finally decided to arrest him. The order was carried out on July 21, 1781. He was imprisoned in the terrible "Piombi"; four years later he succeeded in escaping—an exploit equalled only by Casanova. Henceforth he was to wander throughout Italy, exiled from Venice, then from Naples and Genoa. In 1797 his life came to a tragic end at Bormio.

His wife, Virginia Lechi-Conforte, resided at the villa until 1786, followed by his brother Faustino. Much different from Galeano, Faustino was a lover of the arts, collecting paintings and musical instruments. On November 3, 1772, he very probably received Mozart and his father Leopold, who spoke of him as "an excellent violinist and a much enlightened music lover."

The Austro-Russian invasion of 1799 obliged the Lechi to leave Montirone and seek refuge at Genoa, then in France. The villa was sacked. Count Faustino died at Genoa in 1800 and until 1814 his fortune remained undivided among his numerous children. The Lechi were rather liberal and had enthusiastically adopted the new doctrines of the French Revolution. Giacomo became a member of the Legislative Assembly of the Cisalpine Republic, deputy at the Lyons Council, and finally a member of the legislative body of the Italian Republic. Faithful to his republican ideas, he refused the posts offered by Napoleon in the new Kingdom of Italy, retired from political life and devoted himself to study and literature. Stendhal, who knew him in 1811, described him as "a very graceful man, perfectly natural; but in no way that French grace where one can easily see the joy of well playing a brilliant role, if not even the pride of playing it: here it is graceful grace, simple, pure. This man can be a king or a bourgeois with equal ease." One of his sisters, Francesca, married to Count Francesco Gherardi, also attracted the attention of Stendhal, who judged her "the most fascinating being with the most beautiful eyes one had ever seen perhaps." He went on to say that "Countess Gherardi, daughter of Count Lechi, perhaps had the most beautiful eyes in Brescia, the country of beautiful eyes. I have never seen the most tender beauty combined with the most unusual genius as in Madame Gherardi, one of the wittiest women of this country. To her genius she added a soft gaiety, a real simplicity, which was never altered by the slightest touch of artifice." Countess Gherardi enjoyed a most brilliant position in the Milanese society under the Empire, courted not only by Murat but also by the French minister Petiet.

Several of the Lechi brothers carved out for themselves distinguished careers in the army or in politics. Born in 1778, Teodoro Lechi took part in the rebellion against Venice in 1797 and linked his own fate with that of France. He entered the Italian Legion commanded by his brother Giuseppe, took part in the Italian campaigns, was made commander of the Presidential Guard, then of the Royal Guard, which he led during the battles of Ulm, Austerlitz, during the Dalmatian campaign, at Wagram, then during the Russian campaign.

On the fall of the Empire, he took part in the "Generals' Conspiracy" and was condemned to death. The sentence was commuted and he was imprisoned at Mantua from 1814 to 1818. In 1848, he commanded the militia of the provisional government at Milan and was obliged to emigrate to Piedmont when Austria succeeded in regaining power. Charles Albert of Savoy named him army general. Exile and confiscation of some of his possessions by the Austrian authorities obliged him unfortunately to sell several pieces of his beautiful collections in his villa at Montirone. He finally returned to his domain in 1859 and died seven years later.

Count Giuseppe Lechi, who was born in 1776, also played an important role during the imperial period. Recalling his most valuable collaborators, Napoleon at Elba said: "I had Lechi in Italy." He likewise took part in the Italian campaign, and it was he who raised the Italian Legion. During the capture of Trent he was named brigadier general. His daring deeds were already legendary. "During the time of Marengo," wrote Stendhal, "Italy had but a single man who dared to march to the cannon, General Lechi." He aided Murat at Milan from 1801

*Countess Francesca Gherardi*

to 1803, took part in the Apulian campaign, then in that of Naples with Joseph Bonaparte. In 1808 he was in Catalonia and was named military governor of Barcelona; he distinguished himself at the capture of Gerona in 1809. The Spaniards called him "the devil on the white horse." In 1813 he found Murat again at Naples. As Governor of Tuscany in 1814 he, together with Joseph Fouché, signed the Lucca Convention. Named governor of Apulia shortly afterward, he came to Murat's aid in his attempt to save his throne. After the defeat he was handed over to the Austrians and condemned to three years' imprisonment in a fortress. On regaining his freedom, he divided his time until his death in 1836 between his villa at Montirone and his palace at Brescia.

He had married the daughter of Count Siméon, but they had no children. He bequeathed his Montirone domain to his adopted daughter Elisa, who married Count Francesco Longo. Their heiress, Countess Elena Agliardi, sold Montirone in 1883 to Countess Giulia Lechi, widow of Faustino Lechi and daughter-in-law of Count Teodoro. Countess Giulia's descendant, Antonio Lechi, still possesses this beautiful dwelling.

## Calino *Villa Maggi*

Taking part in 1148 in the siege of Damascus under the command of the Emperor Conrad III of Hohenstaufen and Louis VII, King of France, Geri di Calino, lord of the territory of Calino, the site of the present villa Maggi, was the first man to raise the standard of the Crusaders on the city walls. In reward for this great deed, the Emperor allowed him to include in his coat-of-arms a gold ladder and a silver standard against an azure background; these arms have been preserved by his descendants. They took the name of Calino, being the originators, and later settled at Brescia, where they were admitted into the city's patriciate. Various partitions occasioned by successions divided the family's possessions. Ottino Calino, treasurer to the Duke Filippo Maria Visconti, was at Calino in 1430.

*Members of the Maggi family*

A castle stood at Calino from at least the fourteenth century and without doubt well before; it was in ruins when Vicenzo Calino decided in 1697 to replace it with the present villa. Construction was finished in 1706. That same year, Vicenzo Calino, who was attached to the court of Tuscany and had been made count by the Grand Duke, received at the villa Maximilian, Elector of Bavaria.

Count Rutilio Calino, son of Count Vicenzo who died in 1710, laid out the gardens of the villa and with the aid of his brother, Cardinal Ludovico Calino, erected in the village the Church of San Stefano, where the family tombs are found. Count Rutilio, his wife Countess Elena Avogadro and their sons led a sumptuous life at the villa which caused the Brescians to remark that "there was always open house at Calino."

The sons of Count Rutilio lived to a very old age and left no descendants. The last of them, Count Filippe, died in 1820 at the age of eighty-nine, bequeathing his domains to his cousin, Count Rutilio di Muzio, who had sided with Napoleon and had been made Baron of the Kingdom of Italy and Knight of the Iron Crown, while his wife was lady in waiting to the Queen of Italy. Their children, Ludovico and Muzio, unfortunately offered them nothing but disappointment: the first died before they did, after an unsuitable marriage, the second, although a man of culture and friend of the poet and novelist Alessandro Manzoni, was strange and slightly unbalanced, leaving the villa in an utter state of abandonment.

When he died in 1874, his grand nephew, Count Bernardo Maggi della Gradella, acquired possession of the domain and restored the villa, which has remained in the family and is today the property of Countess Camilla Maggi.

*Count Pietro Lechi*

Genoa

# *Palazzo Pallavicini*

The shadows which in the garden soften the warm sunlight of the Italian Riviera are among the great charms of the Palazzo Pallavicini standing in the heart of the city. Piazza Fontana Marose, a loggia, with its cool vaults supported by Tuscan columns, offers a fine view. Statues, busts and jars bursting with luxuriant vegetation heighten the purity of the architectural setting by their elegance. The Palazzo Pallavicini, built from 1565 to 1575 by the architect Francesco Casella on vestiges of a more ancient edifice, was largely restored in the mid-nineteenth century.

The entrance vestibule (*above*) in its present state is the fruit of two working campaigns carried out at different periods. The frescoes of the vault date from the construction of the palace and were painted about 1575 by the brothers Benedetto and Panatelo Calvi. They represent in the center an episode in the story of Joshua and, in the voussoirs, figures and allegorical and Biblical scenes. The mural decoration of the pilasters and arabesques in the Renaissance taste was executed from 1844 to 1852 from designs by the architect Pittaluga. The statue of Helen was executed in 1854 by Salvatore Revelli, and below the large staircase, also in a niche, is an older statue of Antinous Niccolò Traverso (dating from the close of the eighteenth century).

Shimmering in its crystal beauty, a huge chandelier dominates the grand salon *(right page)* whose mural decoration in the neo-classic style dates from the mid-nineteenth century. Very much restrained yet warm, owing to the rich use of gold, marble and silk, the setting emphasizes even more the magnificently Baroque style of the two Genoese consoles dating from the latter half of the seventeenth century, which are adorned with figures of children emerging from a forest of volutes and garlands. The tapestry which represents Spring was made in Flemish workshops during the sixteenth century. An important collection of Far Eastern ceramics, including two superb Chinese porcelain eagles, is symmetrically arranged on the consoles and the table in the foreground.

The Palazzo Doria Principe originally stood beyond the walls of the city of Genoa. It was in fact a country residence, a villa situated in the midst of vast gardens which, as shown in the engraving below, extended on the one hand before the palace, toward the sea, and on the other were laid out in terraces behind, on the hill dominating the gulf. The rear section of the garden, however, is now covered by modern constructions. All that exists on the crest of the hill is a colossal statue of Jupiter erected on the tomb of a dog presented to Andrea Doria by Charles V. In front of the palace there was once a landing stage reserved for Doria's galleys; today the construction of the maritime station of Genoa has spoiled the view of the gardens.

A venerable old man, Prince of Melfi, Knight of the Golden Fleece, "father and liberator" of his country, Andrea Doria *(right)* had himself

# *Palazzo Doria Principe*

painted when he was well on in age, facing the viewer, with a mysterious cat which clearly shows signs of uneasiness. According to tradition, the animal was the emblem of the Fieschi who, in 1547, made an unsuccessful attempt to attack the all-powerful admiral. It was Andrea Doria who built the Palazzo Doria Principe very probably from designs by Domenico Caranca. The architect had to consider an earlier edifice which formed the central part of the present palace and was obviously remodelled. Work lasted from 1521 to 1529, but additions were made after Andrea Doria's death by his nephew Giannandrea. The gardens designed by Fra Montorsoli were famous. A pupil of Raphael, Perino del Vaga, driven from Rome after the sack of the city, decorated several rooms of the palace in 1528, especially the Room of the Giants, where we see on the ceiling *(following double page) Jupiter Crushing the Titans* — an obvious allusion to Andrea's power and to the fate awaiting his enemies, as well as a pretext for the artist to display his knowledge of anatomy.

# *Palazzo Durazzo-Pallavicini*

Characteristic in its magnificent size of the great Genoese dwellings of the sixteenth and seventeenth centuries, the entrance vestibule (*left page*) leads by means of a huge staircase to the inner courtyard enclosed on the ground floor by an open portico. A host of columns support the vaults, but there is no ornamentation to alter the architectural purity of the design. The palace was begun in 1618 from the designs by Bartolomeo Bianco, one of the great Genoese architects, who also designed the Palazzo Balbi-Serangea, the Reggia and the University, close by in the Via Balbi. The Palazzo Durazzo-Pallavicini was modified about 1778-1780 by the architect Andrea Tagliafichi, who placed the statue of *Fidelity* by Francesco Ravaschio and that of *Force* by Niccolò Traverso below the vestibule steps. Tagliafichi also added to the façade facing the Via Balbi two loggias (one of which is shown above) adorned with a graceful stucco decoration. Through the arcades we can see the façade of the ancient Church of Saint Jerome and Saint Francis Xavier erected in 1658 probably by Corradi.

The series of salons of the Palazzo Durazzo-Pallavicini contains the most important private collection in Genoa. Certainly the most famous painting is the *Boy in White Satin* by Van Dyck *(right page,* left of the door), considered the masterpiece of his Genoese period. Above the door is *Christ Appearing to the Virgin* by Domenichino, who also painted the *Venus Weeping Over the Death of Adonis* which hangs to the left of Van Dyck's *Boy in White Satin.* The canvases have been integrated into a *trompe-l'œil* décor which, like the ceiling fresco by Paolo Gerolamo Piola, dates from the close of the seventeenth century.

The same arrangement was used for the small salon *(above)* whose décor, executed much later in the early nineteenth century, is also more restrained. The large painting by Jan Bruegel on the far wall, representing *The Empire of Flora,* is surmounted by two landscapes by painters of the seventeenth-century Flemish School. On the right wall, above a triptych by Lucas van Leyden, is Franceschini's *Mary Magdalene Carried Off by Angels.*

# *Palazzo del Tè*

A simple villa designed for the diversions and fêtes of the court of Federigo Gonzaga, the Palazzo del Tè consists of only four main buildings without additional stories enclosing a square courtyard. The reverse façade *(above)* opens by means of a loggia onto the gardens (*right page*) and terminates in an exedra with semicircular arcades. Construction was begun in 1524 and the buildings were completed two years later. Palazzo del Tè had at that time excited great interest. The rustic, regular embossed stonework of the courtyard and of the central portico of the loggia with its arcades supported by columns was a theme shortly afterwards used by Palladio.

"One cannot imagine a painting more horrible and frightening than this one," wrote Vasari in reference to the Sala dei Giganti (Room of the Giants) where Giulio Romano had portrayed the fall of the Titans after they were crushed by the gods of Olympus. Although the entire room creates the impression of gigantic turmoil that is almost stupefying in its impact, it is evident that Giulio Romano's talent as a painter was inferior to his gifts as architect and decorator. The Titans with their exaggerated anatomy and their grimacing faces seem to be caricatures when compared with the heroic muscular figures of Michelangelo, while the gods, painted in a frigid academic manner, are far removed from Raphael's models on which they were evidently based. Nevertheless the Sala dei Giganti is interesting historically as one of the first examples of the Mannerist style which was to enjoy a great success in Italy in the second half of the sixteenth century and all of the seventeenth century.

The Gonzaga stud farms were famous throughout sixteenth-century Europe and the horses foaled there were very much appreciated as diplomatic gifts in foreign courts. The Sala dei Cavalli *(below)* preserves the memory of the finest horses of the ducal stables, represented life size by Rinaldo Mantovano in a splendid *trompe-l'œil* architectural decoration executed from designs by Giulio Romano. The statues, the busts, the bas-reliefs alternate with pilasters on a background of imitation colored marble. The wooden coffer ceiling is a splendid architectural achievement. A heart-rending stab of melancholy now strikes the visitor to this superb setting, once a glittering example of grandeur but now uninhabited.

# *Reggia*

"La prima donna del mondo" (the first lady of the world)—such was the title poets and courtiers fawningly bestowed on Isabella d'Este, Marquise of Mantua (*left page*). In fact, more than any of her contemporaries, she personified the Renaissance ideal in a period when illustrious rivals were in no way lacking. Born in 1474 at the court of Ferrara, daughter of Duke Ercole I and Eleanor of Aragon, married in 1490 to Francesco Gonzaga, Marquis of Mantua, she was the sister of Beatrice d'Este, wife of Ludovico il Moro, the sister-in-law of Lucrezia Borgia, Duchess of Ferrara, and of Elizabeth Gonzaga, Duchess of Urbino. While visiting Mantua in January-February of 1500, Leonardo da Vinci is said to have made a pencil portrait of her (reproduced here) which is in the Louvre. Although its attribution has been contested and there is controversy about the identity of the model, one would very much like to believe that this fine face with its meditative and pleasant expression is really that of the incomparable Isabella herself.

An enormous building covering an area of almost ten acres and containing more than five hundred rooms, the Reggia or ducal palace consists of various constructions erected from the beginning of the fourteenth century to the close of the sixteenth. The Castello San Giorgio (*above*) protects the ensemble with its massive square towers crowned by machicolation and commands a fine view over the lakes surrounding the city. The Castello was erected in 1395 by the architect Bartolino Novara and then became the residence of the marquises of Mantua. It was here that Isabella d'Este, from the time of her marriage in 1490 until her widowhood in 1523, had her apartments and her famous "studiolo" where she enjoyed collecting art objects, incunabula and splendid paintings.

Writing about Mantua, Aldous Huxley said: "I have seen dead or decadent cities, but nowhere else was desolation heavier with the memory of its splendor." And in fact a feeling of somber melancholy emanates from the Palazzo del Capitano, whose austere plain brick façade with dark arcades on the ground floor dates from the very beginning of the fourteenth century. When Luigi Gonzaga seized Mantua in 1328 after driving out the Bonascolsi, who were then masters, by means of a popular uprising, he decided to settle here. The Palazzo del Capitano is therefore the origin of the Reggia. Gradually other constructions were added until finally it formed a rather vast ensemble. In 1459, when Ludovico transferred the princely apartments to the Castello San Giorgio, these constructions became known as the "Corte Vecchia."

A gigantic pergola, the Room of the Rivers *(below)*, is entirely decorated with trellis work covered with vines which extends from the walls to the vault. In the arcades are figures symbolizing various Italian rivers after which the room is named. The decoration, entirely of *trompe-l'œil,* was executed in 1776 by Giorgi Anselmi on the order of the Empress Maria Theresa—then sovereign of Mantua—who is represented, in the central medallion of the ceiling, as Euterpe, the Muse of Music, surrounded by rays on a throne of clouds. The far end of the gallery is occupied by a rock grotto containing a neo-classic urn dating from the early nineteenth century.

During the years 1461 to 1474, Mantegna decorated the Camera degli Sposi (the room in honor of the marriage of Ludovico Gonzaga and Barbara of Brandenburg) whose splendid frescoes are perhaps the most remarkable ensemble to have come down to us from the Quattrocento. The subject matter assigned to the artist deals with an important event in Ludovico's life—the nomination of his son Francesco to the cardinalate. Above the fireplace (*left page*) the marquis is portrayed surrounded by his family receiving the announcement of the happy event. Between the two doors he is shown greeting the new cardinal on his return from Rome. The painter did not hesitate to portray the figures with scrupulous exactitude: the marquis and his wife were ugly and several of their children had inherited from their Malatesta grandmother a pronounced deviation of the spinal column. The portraits, however, are psychologically penetrating and the nobility of their attitude gives them an outstanding monumental quality. In the background Mantegna revealed himself an astonishing landscape artist, as we can see in a hunting scene (*opposite right*) and also in the remarkable decorative composition in the vault. In its center, enclosed by architectural motifs, arabesques, medallions and garlands of flowers, is an oculus revealing an intensely blue sky splashed with sunlight and full of Cupids and birds.

Bogliaco

# *Villa Bettoni*

Utilizing the slopes of the hill which rise around Lake Garda and fronted by the flanks of the Alps, the gardens of the villa are spread out in a series of terraces connected by flights of steps, leading to a central opening which, in the original project, led to a temple dedicated to Apollo (*see also the following double page*). Grottoes, niches, statues of women and children, the work of the sculptor Gianbattista Locatelli, along with vases and balustrades enliven the magnificently theatrical character of the composition. On either side of the terraces are lemon tree gardens which in winter are converted into greenhouses by covering them with panes of glass. Semicircular grilles separate the villa, whose other façade faces the lake, and the gardens which were finished about 1760.

The public and domestic virtues of the Bettoni, symbolized by Locatelli's statues of gods and goddesses, mythological heroes and heroines, greet the visitor along the entire staircase *(following double page)*. At the foot of the steps industrious Mercury with his wand is pendant to wise Minerva *(not shown here)*, while on the first landing Hercules and Omphale, with the club and lionskin of Nemea borrowed from her husband, refer to conjugal love. These are followed by martial boldness reflected in the features of Mars and beauty in those of Venus. Diana, goddess of the hunt, and Apollo, god of the arts *(not shown here)*, end the procession. This sumptuous and elegant staircase, designed by the architect Abbot Antonio Marchetti, was executed in 1758. The artist Beniamino Gallari —who later carved out a career for himself at Berlin in the service of Frederick II—painted the *trompe-l'œil* decoration which covers the walls: in one niche we find an imperious Juno accepting the homage of a peacock, while a young woman gazes with curiosity at this surprising spectacle.

# *Villa Lechi*

Montirone

The villa (*above*) consists of a central main building, crowned by an attic story, and two small loggias from which extend two wings at right angles, delimiting a courtyard enclosed by pilasters and grilles. This façade faces a garden laid out in the Italian style with box trees framing an artificial lake. The simplicity of this edifice, built from 1739 to 1744, offers no inkling on the exterior of the delightful Rococo decoration within. The staircase with its banister adorned with figures of children and a stone lion leads to a gallery of honor (*left page*) entirely painted in fresco with architectural motifs framing on the ceiling and walls such allegorical and mythological figures as Apollo, Aurora, War, Music and Poetry. The figures are by the great decorator Carlo Carloni, the architectural motifs by Giacomo Lecchi. The central medallion of the ceiling, destroyed during bombardment in 1943, has been reconstructed. More astonishing still is the ballroom *(following double page)* which in 1746 was entirely decorated in *trompe-l'œil* by the same artist. The vast arcades open on to architectural compositions very similar to those found in the theatrical decorations of the great period and which reveal an unusual mastery of perspective. The gentilhomme who is proudly descending the monumental staircase with his companion is none other than Pietro Lechi depicted in the act of presenting to his wife the splendid salon executed on his order.

Calino

# *Villa Maggi*

A triumph of illusion, the villa, which was built from 1697 to 1706, is entirely painted both on the exterior and interior with a simulated architectural decoration which is still perfectly preserved in the apartments. The framework of a door leading to one of the rooms *(above)*, flanked by columns, consists of a majestic pediment, the whole executed in *trompe-l'œil*. The window recess is covered with a series of portraits, dating for the most part from the nineteenth century and representing various members of the Maggi family, who still own the domain. On the very simple façades *(right)*, the enormous cartouches with coats-of-arms placed between the windows, the rinceaux frieze running along the attic story, with their patina partly worn away by bad weather, have acquired a faded color and softness emphasized even more by the Lombard green vegetation.

# *Tuscany and the Marches*

*With its villas, its parks, its terraced gardens studded with delightful statues among cypress and pine trees, Tuscany is the most privileged region of Italy. Its pleasant, harmonious landscapes and its fertile soil have given its inhabitants that refined and measured artistic instinct which reached its zenith during the Renaissance. Standing on the banks of the Arno, Florence, which in the fifteenth century was the first industrial city, the most important financial center and the intellectual capital of Europe, is rich in memories of the Medici family. Ruling until 1737, this dynasty of patron-bankers made Tuscany a prosperous state and left it an incomparable artistic patrimony of which it is proud. In 1738 François de Lorraine became Grand Duke of Tuscany, henceforth and until 1859 the Hapsburgs occupied the Pitti Palace. Yet the Bourbons (1801-1807) and Elisa Bonaparte (1807-1814) ruled in their place. Finally in 1865 Florence was destined for a few years to become the capital of the young Kingdom of Italy.*

*East of Tuscany the Marches consist of steep valleys bordered by a long and sterile strip of sand eaten away by the sea. In the center Urbino, thanks to the Montefeltro, was for more than a century to play a role as brilliant as that of Florence. But the destiny of the principality was short-lived and in 1631 it fell into papal hands.*

## Florence *Palazzo Corsini*

On the site of the present palace once stood the dwellings of the Compagni, the Aldinghelli and the Segmi, acquired by Maria Maddalena Macchiavelli, rich heiress and wife of Filippo Corsini, in 1649. The Corsini were members of one of the most illustrious Italian families. Originally from Oiggibonsi, in the province of Siena, Neri Corsini had settled at Florence about 1170. His descendants included Andrea Corsini (1302-1373) who died as bishop of Fiesole, surrounded by public veneration, and was canonized in 1629. The Corsini had a brilliant career at Florence, where they actively participated in civic life and held important posts in the Republic. In 1371 Filippo Corsini, ambassador at twenty-six, received from Emperor Charles IV the title of Palatine Count. Finally in 1730 Cardinal Lorenzo Corsini was elected Pope as Clement XII. A year later his nephew was named Roman Prince and in 1732 grandee. Shortly after his election the Pope became blind and had to allow his other nephew, Cardinal Corsini, to administer his possessions. Charles de Brosses, who saw him during his journey to Italy, complaining of his bad state of affairs, recorded his lament: "I was a rich abbot, a well-off prelate, a poor cardinal and a ruined pope."

The Corsini Palace at Florence had been erected during the final quarter of the seventeenth century by the Pope's older brother, Marquis Filippo Corsini, on the site of the dwellings acquired by his grandmother in 1649. The marquis had been the friend of Cosimo II de' Medici and during his youth had traveled with him in Europe. His travel chronicles together with drawings are now kept in the Laurentian Library at Florence, and reveal his artistic taste and curiosity. The architect who designed the palace was Pier Francesco Silvani.

Marie-Madeleine *School of Rubens*

In the nineteenth century Neri Corsini, Marquis of Lajatico (1805-1859), great grandfather of the present owner of the palace, was one of the leaders of the Florentine liberal party. During the uprising of 1848 he was named minister and had to flee Piedmont when the Grand Duke Leopold II regained power. In 1856 when the latter was threatened with a new revolution, he tried in vain to grant full power to Neri Corsini, who refused. But three years later he was sent on a mission to London by the provisional Tuscan government.

*Cardinal Neri Corsini*

The palace and its very beautiful collection of paintings are now the property of Prince Tommaso Corsini.

## Giogoli *Villa dei Collazzi*

"If one gathered in a single enclosure and under the same name your (Florence's) palaces scattered in the countryside, you would not be far from equalling two Romes," wrote Ariosto in regard to the innumerable villas surrounding Florence. Among these the Villa dei Collazzi certainly ranks as one of the most perfect and intact. Work was begun at a date difficult to determine precisely, about the middle of the sixteenth century, by Agostino Dini della Libertà, descended from a rich banking family, on a piece of land that had been acquired by his family in 1427 from Lodovico Bonaventuri and which had formerly belonged to the Buondelmonte. Which architect designed the villa? The question is still debated. According to tradition the design was made by Michelangelo, while Santi di Tito directed the construction and above all the decoration.

The edifice was both a summer residence and a main house for a farming venture. The ancient wine press can still be seen here and, in the cellars, the earthenware jars with the arms of the Dini family in which oil was kept. Close to the seignorial dwelling was a small village where those who worked in the fields, vineyards and olive groves lived. The villa was never finished and the left wing was not completed until recently.

In 1719 another Agostino Dini married a rich heiress, Maria Medea Castelli, who in 1735 commissioned the painter Menucci, the pupil of Sebastiano Ricci, to decorate the chapel with frescoes. In 1754 she replaced the staircase which leads to the terrace by the double flight of steps which can still be seen. The marriage in 1782 of Giovanni Dini, ambassador to Moscow, to a young Russian named Maria Buturline, contributed even more to the beauty of the setting, for she had the park planted with handsome holm oaks, pine and cypress trees which despite serious damage during fighting in 1944 are among the charms of the villa.

In the mid-nineteenth century the Dini sold the villa to the Bombicci who in 1899 received the Empress Victoria of Germany. In 1918 the domain passed into the hands of Carlo and Guido Chierichetti, then was sold again in 1933. The new owners are completing the construction with great care, following the original design and using the same building materials available in the sixteenth century.

## Marlia *Villa Reale*

In 1817, after a visit to Italy, the Austrian diplomat and statesman Prince Metternich wrote about the gardens of the Villa Reale: "I know of no other on this side of the Alps with such luxuriant trees and exotic flowers." And he congratulated himself on this "truly divine" sojourn in a dwelling comparable to "the most comfortable chateaux in France."

This enchanting place was partly the work of Elisa Bonaparte, Napoleon's sister, who, in 1805, had been named Princess of Lucca and of Piombino—titles and estates rather modest for her taste. On July 5, 1806, she purchased from Count Lelio Orsetti, ex-chamberlain of the Queen of Etruria, the domain of Marlia for the enormous sum of 128,000 Luccan écus or more than 700,000 francs of the period. She had to add a villa and a park which once belonged to the bishops of Lucca (today they are still a part of this domain) and which were visited by Montaigne during his journey to Italy. The funds necessary for the acquisition had been taken largely from the ecclesiastical reserves of the principality which Elisa was eager to seize.

At Marlia she found splendid gardens and a huge villa dating from the close of the seventeenth century. She at once enlarged the domain by purchasing the neighboring lands; she laid out a garden in the English style and remodelled the interior and exterior of the villa. The furniture was partly crafted by local cabinetmakers. But Elisa did not fail to clamor for imperial furniture to be sent her and to complain loudly when she received only threadbare carpets and unmatched service. She held a brilliant court at her Marlia "palace" and her musical director—with the rank of captain of the guard—was none other than the illustrious Paganini, who was not beneath playing a duet with Félix Bacciochi, the princess' husband. But Bacciochi filled only a secondary role in Elisa's life, for Signore de Cenami, whom she had made Grand Master of the Horse, was the recipient of her affections. The Emperor's sister adorned the theater and often acted herself, chancing her talent not only in such comedies as Louis Benoît Picard's *La Petite Ville* but also in the great tragic roles of Andromache and Phaedra. Paganini played among the clumps of trees and in the verdant theater and his "diabolical" talent is said to have made Elisa faint. These diversions, however, did not prevent her from paying careful attention to the administration of her estates, a task in which she revealed herself to be a woman of authority and competence, deserving—the expression is Talleyrand's—the title of "Semiramis of Lucca." Marlia was the birthplace of Napoleone Bacciochi, the future Countess Camerata, immortalized in Rostand's *L'Aiglon*.

*Prince Felix Bacciochi*

*Elisa Bonaparte*

The year 1814—Elisa was then Grand Duchess of Tuscany—marked the fall of the Napoleonic dynasty. The Duchy of Lucca was given to the Bourbons of Parma, who were waiting to regain their Parma estates, where Marie-Louise, ex-empress of the French, was to reign until her death. In 1820 the villa was the scene of the wedding of Duke Charles-Louis and Maria Theresa of Savoy, in the presence of the bridegroom's father, Victor Emmanuel I, King of Sardinia. When the Kingdom of Italy was created, Marlia became Crown property.

King Victor Emmanuel II granted the property to the widow of the Prince of Capua, whose marriage to a young Englishwoman had not been recognized by the Bourbons of the Two Sicilies. The son resulting from this union suddenly became mad and was institutionalized for thirty years until 1919. At the close of the nineteenth century John Singer Sargent did two watercolors of the large ornamental lake. In 1923 the villa was acquired by Count and Countess Pecci-Blunt—the latter, niece of Pope Leo XIII, is the present owner—who completely restored the building as well as the park surrounding it.

## Segromigno *Villa Mansi*

According to legend, on stormy nights a radiantly beautiful woman dressed entirely in white can be seen roaming about the Villa Mansi and this, we are told, is none other than the ghost of Lucida Mansi. Born in 1606, the young woman, widow of Vincenzo Diversi, chose Gaspero Mansi for her second husband in 1635. When he died in 1648, she became involved in a number of amorous adventures which created a scandal. A trap door said to be concealed in the floor enabled her lover to leave after satisfying her. She was extremely vain, and it is said that she delighted in the endless reflection of her beauty in the mirrors which covered the walls of her apartment where, completely nude, she would turn about in circles for hours at a time. Then one day the first wrinkles began to appear and Lucida was plunged into the greatest grief. But a strikingly handsome man suddenly appeared. This was, of course, the devil, who said to her: "I have loved you for twenty years, Lucida, and I am waiting for you. Grant me your soul and for thirty years you will remain just as beautiful and desirable." The pact was concluded and time appeared to leave no mark on Lucida's face or body. But thirty years later the young man reappeared . . . and those close to Lucida found her corpse in the room of mirrors, crawling with worms.

The truth is less romantic. Records in the parish church of Sant' Antonio of Lucca reveal that Lucida Mansi died of the plague in 1658, fortified for her eternal journey with the rites of the Church. During this period, however, the villa did not belong to the Mansi family. It had been built in the sixteenth century by the Benedetti, who sold it

*Lucida Mansi*

in 1599 to the Cenami. Originally it was probably a rather simple rectangular structure which Countess Felice Cenami and her brother-in-law, abbot Paolo Cenami, enlarged and completely redecorated in 1634-1635 from the design by the architect Muzio Oddi. In 1675 the villa was acquired by Ottavio Mansi, a member of a very ancient family originally from Silesia who had been settled in Lucca since the High Middle Ages. It was here in 1692 that he received the future Frederick IV of Denmark. Fresh embellishments were given to the exterior of the edifice in 1742 from the design of the abbot Giovanni Francesco Giusti by order of Ottavio Guido Mansi who on two earlier occasions, in 1725 and 1732, had the gardens laid out by Filippo Juvara (they were remodelled in the English style in the early nineteenth century).

Ascanio and Raffaello Mansi were respectively chamberlain and knight of honor of Elisa Bonaparte, Princess of Lucca, and in 1805 the second was delegated as special envoy to the emperor. The Villa Mansi has since remained the property of their descendants and today belongs to Signora Laura Salom Mansi.

Florence

## *Pitti Palace*

"Cosimo de' Medici tells me that you are capable of turning the world around," wrote Pope Eugene IV to Brunelleschi, the architect of the dome of the Cathedral of Santa Maria del Fiore. Brunelleschi replied, "Give me a place to work and I will prove it to you." Such was the manner of man chosen by Lucca Pitti about 1440 to design the palace that he wanted to erect on the left bank of the Arno. After accumulating an enormous banking fortune, Pitti found himself one of the richest men of Florence. His adherence to the party of Cosimo de' Medici had certainly favored his career. After Cosimo's death, however, he had the unfortunate idea of hatching a plot against his son and successor, Piero. He placed himself at the head of the party known as the "Proggio," or "of the hill," and in September, 1466, aided by the gonfalonier Niccolò Soderini, attempted to have the populace make him master. The plot failed; Piero succeeded in having his mandate renewed for a period of ten years and Luca Pitti went into exile where he died in obscurity.

The palace, whose construction was begun by Francelli, was unfinished and remained so until 1549 when Eleonora of Toledo, wife of Duke Cosimo I, acquired it. She commissioned Bartolomeo Ammanati to arrange the inner courtyard. The work, undertaken in 1560, two years after the princess' death, was finished in 1577; in 1569 Cosimo was made Grand Duke by Pius V. Henceforth the grand dukes of Tuscany were to make the Pitti Palace their chief residence.

Francesco I de' Medici succeeded his father in 1574. He is famous for his passion for Bianca Capello, a Venetian adventuress whom he placed on the grand ducal throne. While young, Bianca had been seduced by an employee of a branch of the Salbiati bank in Venice, Pietro Bonaventuri, who married her to escape her family's fury. He asked her to flee with him to Florence after stealing precious objects from the paternal household. At Florence, Bianca soon attracted the attention of Francesco de' Medici, then the princely heir, and became his mistress, while Cosimo negotiated the wedding of his son with the archduchess Joan of Austria. The wedding in no way interrupted the liaison. On the contrary, now residing in a sumptuous dwelling, Bianca retained her status of official mistress while her husband was made chief of the duke's wardrobe. Although complaisant, her husband soon revealed himself to be a man of insufferable character. He seduced a beautiful Florentine, Alessandra Bonciani, widow of a Ricci. The girl's family was scandalized and had the seducer assassinated, quite certainly with the approval of the princely heir. When the latter finally ascended the throne, he freed himself of his marital ties and utterly abandoned his wife, who had borne him only daughters, one of whom, Marie, was to marry Henri IV. Bianca busied herself with settling the dynastic problem since the throne would fall to Francesco's brother, Cardinal Ferdinand de' Medici, her mortal enemy, if there were no male heir. Her licentiousness having made her barren, she pretended to be pregnant, and on the night of August 29, 1576, secretly "had" a child, reputed to be the bastard son of the grand duke. Shortly afterward, those who had been witness to this ruse mysteriously disappeared.

In that year of 1576 Francesco's family was overcome by one tragedy after another. His younger brother, half mad, strangled his young wife Dianora of Toledo, his elder sister, who had married Paolo Giordano Orsini, Duke of Bracciano, took as her lover one of her husband's cousins and was strangled by her outraged husband.

On April 11, 1578, Joan of Austria died—a natural death. Two months later Francesco secretly married Bianca. For the sake of decency the marriage was not declared until a year later at which time Bianca was solemnly crowned during splendid festivities. Her triumph, however, was not complete, for she never succeeded in giving Francesco a legitimate heir. Montaigne, who saw her in 1580 during his journey to Italy, described her as "a beautiful woman after the Italian taste, with a countenance at once pleasing and dignified, of generous build and with opulent breasts." Some years later, in October, 1587, during a hunt at Poggio a Caiano, Francesco and Bianca died within a day of each other, probably of malaria, although Cardinal Ferdinand was suspected of having poisoned them.

No sooner had he mounted the throne than Ferdinand was eager to get rid of his cardinal's hat and, in 1589, he married Christine de Lorraine, granddaughter of Catherine de' Medici.

Cardinal at the age of fourteen, Ferdinand had long lived at Rome where, in 1576, he had purchased the villa of Cardinal Ricci. He finished and partly transformed it. Henceforth it was known as the Villa Medici. Intelligent and tolerant, he made Tuscany prosperous again and enabled the House of Medici to regain the popularity it had lost during the previous reign.

When he died in 1609, his eldest son Cosimo II was only nineteen. He soon allowed himself to be dominated by the monks and the religious party and his reign was scarcely a happy one. Nevertheless, he recognized the merits of Galileo whom he invited to Florence in 1610 and named him "mathematician supraextraordinary" and "philosopher of his most serene grand duke." It was he who in 1620 commissioned the architect Parigi to enlarge the Pitti Palace.

His son, Ferdinand II, although gentle and gracious, was scarcely more brilliant than he was. Ferdinand's wife, the grand duchess Vittoria della Rovere, had a difficult and haughty character and after several years together the couple lived separate lives. However, she contributed to the Medici heritage the wealth of the dukes of Urbino, especially their wonderful collection of art. It was during Ferdinand's reign that the apartments on the first floor of the Pitti Palace were entrusted to Pietro da Cortona, who sumptuously decorated the ceilings. On the advice of his brother Leopold—cardinal in 1667—a great lover of art, the collections of the Medici and those of the della Rovere were exhibited, partly at the Pitti Palace and partly at the Uffizi, which was then made into a museum.

*The Boboli Gardens at the Pitti Palace*

During the same period, probably influenced by the cardinal, the grand duke founded the "Conversazione Filosofica del Palazzo," an academy of sorts where writers and scientists including Evangelista Torricelli gathered to meet at the palace. Leopold personally instituted the "Academia del Cimento" or Proof Academy, a meeting place for scientists, whose remarkable experiments excited great interest. Ferdinand built up an important library at the Pitti Palace known as the "Palatine" to distinguish it from the Laurentian library of the early Medici. He was unable, however, to prevent Galileo's being summoned before the Inquisition in 1633 and the condemnation of his "Dialogo spora i due massimi sistemi del mondo, tolemaico e copernicano."

With the ascension of Cosimo III in 1670, the absurd, tragicomic history of the last Medici began. In 1661 Cosimo had married Marguerite-Louise d'Orléans, daughter of Gaston, the brother of Louis XIII. The marriage had been arranged by Mazarin against the wishes of the princess, who was in love with Duke Charles of Lorraine. The young woman soon adopted an insurmountable antipathy to her husband and this created joy in every European court. The birth of a son in 1663 did not alter matters at all. Ferdinand II was reduced to placing his daughter-in-law under guard at the villa of Poggio a Caiano. When this occurred, Marguerite-Louise burst into a tirade against the grand duke, Italy, the Italians and her husband. "I create your unhappiness and you mine," she declared. "I prefer to go to Hell alone than to paradise with you." Despite these words, she still granted her husband his marital rights, leading to the birth of a daughter, Anna Ludovica, in 1667, and of a second son, Gian Gastone, in 1671. Marguerite-Louise pretended to consider them bastard, since her marriage, she claimed, had been arranged without her consent. Finally, in 1672, his patience exhausted, Cosimo permitted her to leave Tuscany and return to Paris, where she retired to the convent of Picpus. She soon wearied of the place, became friendly with guards and stablemen, and conducted herself so scandalously that Louis XIV ordered her to return to the convent. In order to harass her husband, she wrote him insulting and vitriolic letters. "I swear by what I hate most, that is, you," one of them declared, "that I am making a pact with the devil to drive you mad." She was finally incarcerated at the Convent of Saint-Mandé, where she died, in 1721, at the age of seventy-six.

No sooner had Cosimo II separated from his wife than he set out to assure the Medici succession. His eldest son Fernandino, who was married to Violante Beatrice of Bavaria, died without issue in 1713. His second son, Gian Gastone, had married Anna Maria of Saxe-Lauenbourg, who absolutely refused to leave her principality of Reichstadt, where she dreamed solely of hunting and dogs, for Tuscany; here again the union remained barren. In desperation Cosimo III forced his brother, Cardinal Francesco Maria, to give up the red hat and marry Eleanora Gonzaga in 1709 at the age of fifty. Enormous in size and physically exhausted, Francesco inspired only repulsion in his young wife, and four years later he died childless.

Cosimo ended his long life in a state of bitter despair. Dominated by the religious party, he had spent enormous sums for the "conversion" of heretics, Jews and Protestants. Pensions rewarded those who returned to the Church—pensions ironically called "credo pensions." His only solace at the end was the knowledge that he had enriched his grand ducal collections by adding to the Villa Medici at Rome fine antique statues, including the celebrated Venus de Medici.

*Luca Pitti*

*Francesco de' Medici*

Cosimo III had been ridiculous, his son Gian Gastone was abject. A drunkard and debauchee, he lived in the company of obscure servants who, by catering to his vices, dominated him completely. After dislocating his leg in 1732, he never left his bed in the Pitti Palace until his death in 1737.

By this time the fate of Tuscany had long been discussed in all the European chancelleries. In 1735, after it had been attributed for a time to the Infante Don Carlos, son of Philip V of Spain and of Elizabeth Farnese, the Treaty of Vienna designated it in share to François de Lorraine, husband of Maria Theresa of Austria, who in exchange granted Lorraine to Stanislas Lecinski, Louis XIV's father-in-law. Don Carlos received Naples and Austria received the duchy of Parma. The last of the Medici, Anna Ludovica, widow of the Elector Palatine, occupied one of the wings of the Pitti Palace until her death in 1743. In her will she left the fabulous Medici collections to the new grand duke on condition they never be removed from Tuscany.

François de Lorraine and Maria Theresa took possession of their estates as early as 1739 and lived in the Pitti Palace. On the death of the emperor in

1765, his second son, the future Leopold II, became ruler of Tuscany and remained on the throne until the death of his brother Joseph in 1790. He enlarged the palace by adding the wings at right angles which border the cour d'honneur.

The French Revolution had a strong impact on the fortunes of Tuscany. Ferdinand III, son of Emperor Leopold II, was forced to flee in the face of invasion. From 1801 to 1808 Napoleon made Tuscany a kingdom of Etruria, entrusting it to the son of the Duke of Parma. Annexed by the French empire in 1808, Tuscany was once again raised to a grand duchy for the Emperor's sister Elisa, who held court at the Pitti Palace. Her ephemeral reign was marked by gala evenings including concerts, theatrical performances and grand balls, at one of which, on January 20, 1811, the grand duchess appeared as Clio, the Muse of History, her head crowned with laurel. It was at this time that she ordered the redecoration of several rooms in the apartments and commissioned Antonio Canova to execute his celebrated *Venus Leaving Her Bath.* The sculpture was greeted by the Florentines with tremendous enthusiasm and was destined to replace the Venus de Medici, which had been removed by the French troops in 1799. It still adorns the bathroom used by Elisa Bonaparte.

*Bianca Cappello*

In 1815 Ferdinand II returned to Florence and was succeeded by his son, Grand Duke Leopold II in 1824. In 1819 and 1830, respectively, both sovereigns added to the decoration of the Pitti Palace with a series of ceilings which, alas, suffer cruelly by their proximity to those of Pietro da Cortona. When after a plebiscite Tuscany was reannexed by the kingdom of Italy in 1860, Victor Emmanuel II made Florence his capital; from 1864 to 1870 he resided at the Pitti Palace where he arranged the royal apartments. The palace now belongs to the Italian State and in addition to the Pitti Gallery contains the Goldsmiths Museum, with its Medici treasures, and the Gallery of Modern Art.

## Urbino *Ducal Palace*

In his *Cortigiano*, or ideal of a courtier, Baldassar Castiglione, whose famous portrait by Raphael is now in the Louvre, immortalized the court held at the palace at Urbino by the duchess Elizabeta Gonzaga, the wife of Guidobaldo Montefeltro: "In the evening after dinner it was the habit of all the ladies and gentlemen to go to the apartment of Madame the Duchess. Here in addition to the usual diversions of dancing, comedy and music, curious questions were asked, while other times witty games were invented in which under various imaginary forms each discovered his thoughts. Another time a few disputes were created on different materials and in the heat of the argument each prided himself on fine pat answers, or else mottoes were compared, and there was wonderful pleasure in all these witty games, since the company was made up of fine minds." If we remember that these "fine minds" were, in addition to Castiglione himself, Aretino, the future Cardinal Bibbena, Giulio de' Medici and Pietro Bembo —the latter had received permission from the Pope to read the religious service in Greek in order not to spoil the Ciceronian purity of his Latin— we can understand the influence exerted by the small court at Urbino at the close of the fifteenth century and during the early years of the sixteenth.

Construction of the palace dated from the time of Federigo III, Guidobaldo's father, who had become ruler in 1444 after the assassination of his brother Oddantonio following a conspiracy. The earliest work was undertaken about 1447 with the aid of two Florentine artists: Maso di Bartolomeo for the architecture and Michele di Giovanni for the sculpture. But in 1468 Federigo entrusted the direction of the work to Luciano da Laurana of Dalmatia, who supervised the construction until 1472 and gave it its present aspect. In the sixteenth century a story was added to the palace, thus altering its design.

Federigo was among the most striking personalities of the Italian Renaissance. An accomplished warrior, in order to preserve the sovereignty of his small estates, he was forced successively to serve various lords anxious for his assistance. Thus we find him from 1444 to 1447 at the head of Francesco Sforza's troops, then from 1447 to 1451 in command of those of Florence. He defended Ferdinand I of Naples against Jean d'Anjou and in 1460 won the battle of San Fabiano d'Ascoli. In 1463 he sided with Pius II against Sigismondo Malatesta and was named "Vicar of the Church." At the head of the Italian league, he inflicted a crushing defeat on the Venetian condottiere Colleoni at the battle of Molinella in 1467. Two years later he supported Roberto Malatesta against pope Paul II and in 1472 forced the city of Volterra, which had revolted against Florence, to open its gates after a siege of twenty-five days. In 1474 his brilliant career was crowned with the ducal dignity.

Federigo's military activities did not prevent him from becoming one of the most learned men of his time. He had built up a splendid library whose volumes were uniformly bound in crimson satin enriched with silver ornaments and "out of reach of dirty persons or those lacking in taste," according to the librarian Vespasiano —which leads us to think that access was easy for scholars. Federigo refused to accept any printed book, employing from thirty to forty "scrittori" in recopying not only the works of Sophocles and Pindar but also those of Dante and Boccaccio. He was the patron of Piero della Francesca from whom he commissioned his portrait and that of his second wife (now in the Uffizi at Florence), as well as the *Flagellation*, which is still at the Ducal Palace. He also attracted to his court Justus van Ghent and Pedro Berrugete who decorated his "studiolo."

On his death in 1482 he was succeeded by his son Guidobaldo, the husband of Elizabeta Gonzaga. The "Court of the Muses," praised by Baldassar Castiglione, came to a sudden end during the summer of 1502 when Cesare Borgia seized Urbino. The event plunged the small Italian states in grief. Lucrezia Borgia, the aggressor's sister, wrote that, considering her suffering, she would have preferred not to have known the Duchess of Urbino and "that she would support her as much as she could by words and deeds." Guidobaldo and Elizabeta sought refuge at Mantua, then at Venice, but they regained their estates in 1503 on the death of Pope Alexander VI, father of Cesare Borgia. At Urbino they were greeted by ecstasies of joy, the women of the city holding olive branches. During the carnival which followed on February 19, 1504, a kind of "review" of recent events was given in the palace theater, in which the felony of the Borgia was "vilified" and the grandeur of the Montefeltro was exalted by innumerable allegories.

Being childless, Guidobaldo adopted his nephew Francesco Maria della Rovere who succeeded him in 1508. The following year Francesco Maria married Leonora Gonzaga, daughter of Isabella d'Este. His career also was anything but peaceful. No sooner was he named captain general of the troops of the Church than he incurred the anger of his uncle Julius II for having personally assassinated Cardinal Alidosi, the latter's favorite, but was soon pardoned. The pontificate of Leo X was less favorable. The Medici put forward a claim to chase the della Rovere from Urbino and to obtain the duchy for themselves. The old duchess Elizabeta Gonzaga, who had formerly received the exiled Medici at the Ducal Palace of Urbino, was sent to plead with the Pope. "Has your Holiness forgotten what it is to be driven from one country and forced to wander by begging one's bread?" Her efforts were futile, however, and on August 18, 1516, Lorenzo de' Medici was proclaimed Duke of Urbino and Captain of the Church.

Baldassar Castiglione *by Raphael*

Francesco Maria's exile at Mantua

lasted until the death of Leo X in 1521, at which time he regained possession of his estates. In 1523 he was named general-in-chief of the Venetian troops and died in 1538. He was succeeded by his son Guidobaldo II. His reign was a calmer one, since the duke was more interested in the arts than in warlike exploits. He was the patron of Tasso, commissioned Titian to paint several canvases, including the *Venus of Urbino*, now in the Uffizi, and discussed with Michelangelo the difficult problem of the tomb of Julius II which he had inherited. The heavy expenses in which he became involved caused him in 1572 to increase taxes and this led to a revolt which he harshly repressed.

His son Francesco Maria II was the last Duke of Urbino. He distinguished himself at the battle of Lepanto and left various writings and a correspondence which reveals his culture and lofty thoughts. He had been raised at the Spanish court where he was the friend of the unfortunate Don Carlos, son of Philip II. His first marriage in 1570 to Lucrezia d'Este—fourteen years his senior—the daughter of Ercole II of Ferrara and Renée of France, was not a happy one. In 1577 the duchess left Urbino for Ferrara; her passion for Ercole Contarini ended tragically when he was assassinated by order of Alfonso II d'Este, who was concerned about his sister's honor. In 1599 Francesco Maria married his niece once removed, Livia della Rovere, and had a son, Federigo, who died in 1623, leaving only a daughter. The following year Pope Urban VIII negotiated with the duke, who was then in a quasi-monastic retreat, on the arrangement of the succession of Urbino, with the result that the duke left all his estates to the Pope. On the death of Francesco Maria in 1631 his granddaughter Maria Vittoria inherited the family collections and, on the occasion of her marriage in 1634 to Ferdinand II de' Medici, had the majority transported to Florence, where they are now kept either at the Uffizi or at the Pitti Palace. However, the pope's nephews, the Barberini, seized the manuscripts which are now in the Vatican Library. The furnishings of Federigo's "studiolo" were also transported to Rome and became a part of the Barberini Collection; some of these pieces have been returned to the Ducal Palace at Urbino, while the rest can be seen at the Louvre.

From this time on the Ducal Palace at Urbino was the residence of the cardinal legates. In the eighteenth century it was the residence of the Stuart pretender who was given use of some of the apartments by the pope. In the nineteenth century most of the palace was converted into offices. Since 1881 it has been the home of the Fine Arts Institute of Urbino and the National Gallery of the Marches.

*Battista Sforza, Duchess of Urbino*

*Federigo Montefeltro, Duke of Urbino*

The Venus of Urbino *by Titian*

# *Palazzo Corsini*

Erected on the banks of the Arno, the palace is a huge construction. The long façade facing the river is formed by two wings flanking a courtyard which is closed by a much lower wing containing a portal. At the far end of the courtyard, a pavilion decorated with arcaded loggias dominates the composition. The edifice is unfinished, for the left wing which has only four windows was originally meant to be of the same dimensions as those of the right wing. Construction was undertaken about 1675 for Marquis Filippo Corsini from the design by Pier Francesco Silvani, the architect of the chapel of St. Andrea Corsini in the church of Santa Maria del Carmine. Silvani directed the work until his death in 1685 when he was succeeded by Antonio Ferri.

In his *Italian Hours*, Henry James wrote: "The rooms at the Palazzo Corsini suggest indeed, and seem to recall, but a monotony of peace and plenty. One of them imaged such a noble perfection of a home-scene that I dawdled there until the old custodian came shuffling back to see whether possibly I was trying to conceal a Caravaggio about my person: a great crimson-draped drawing room of the amplest and yet most charming proportions; walls hung with large dark pictures, a great concave ceiling frescoed and moulded with dusky richness, and half-a-dozen south windows looking out on the Arno, whose swift yellow tide sends up the light in a cheerful flicker." The grand salon has scarcely changed since James's visit. On the walls we see a part of the important collection of paintings contained in the palace. In the stucco framework of the ceiling, probably by Giovanni Passardi, Domenico Galliani painted the Virtues supported by Pallas and Mars and crowned by Eternity while Fame sculptures the statue of Hercules; the work was finished in 1700. The furniture of the room dates from the eighteenth century with the exception of the sofas and the pedestal table in the center which date from the nineteenth century.

An arm raised in a gesture of imperious benediction, the statue of Clement XII Corsini, with his pontifical tiara, adorns the landing of the grand staircase, but despite the undeniable quality of the work, the sculptor is unknown. The staircase was erected about 1690 from the design by Antonio Ferri. Both banisters, beginning at the ground floor, lead to the first landing where they join to reach the noble story. The statues dominating the scene have been inspired by classical art. The stucco decoration of the ceiling and of the columns is the work of Giovanni Passardi. The niche containing the statue of the Pope was arranged in 1737 by Girolamo Ticcati, who was probably also responsible for the angels supporting a shield with the arms of the Corsini.

# *Villa dei Collazzi*

A long tradition has credited the architecture of the villa to Michelangelo—a tradition unconfirmed by formal proof yet substantiated by the beauty of the edifice. The artist was a great friend of Agostino Dini, owner of the domain, and he could very well have provided the plans and designs while working at Florence from 1520 to 1530 on the sacristy of San Lorenzo and the Laurentian Library. The construction of the villa probably took place in the second half of the sixteenth century under the direction of Santi di Tito who signed and dated the *Marriage at Cana* which can still be seen in the chapel. The entrance façade (*above*) has in the center a staircase with a twin banister leading to the door, while on the first floor two loggias with three arcades (only one of which is seen here) are arranged symmetrically in relation to the median window. The lateral façade (*opposite right*) owes its beauty to the purity of its design and the harmonious arrangement of its bays. The edifice was finished only recently by its present owners, who also created the handsome basin which we see in the foreground.

From the loggias which adorn the entrance façade (*opposite right*) we can see the Florentine countryside with its gentle hills, its cypresses, its olive groves and its parasol pines, as often represented by the Quattrocento painters. The rhythm of the columns and arcades standing out against the sunny landscape reaches astonishing purity. The villa owes much of its beauty to the materials used in its construction. All the architectonic elements—pediments and window consoles, angle piers (*above*) executed in "pietra serena" of a beautiful dark gray tonality, show up with great precision against the white covered walls.

Opening on to the azure sky, the avenue leading to the villa (*right*) is bordered by splendid cypresses whose dense dark foliage forms two vertiginous walls. On the reverse façade (*above*) three main buildings enclose the terrace overlooking the garden. An arcaded gallery occupies the building at the far end, while a loggia on the story girdles the three sides of the edifice. The perfection of the outline, the balanced design of the windows and columns, establish the entirely Tuscan purity of the composition. The two lions with their skillfully wound manes which support the shield of the Dini at the beginning of the flight of steps descending to the garden date from 1754.

# *Villa Reale*

Marlia

An engraving made from a drawing by Francesco Venturi (*above*) shows the villa as it was in 1775 before the modifications by Elisa Bonaparte in 1806. The princess replaced the tiled roof bordered by an impressive cornice, and placed a portico flat against the façade in order to give it a "Roman look" (*opposite right*). She had intended to furnish it with majestic access banisters, but the collapse of the Empire prevented the execution of her project. The events of 1814 also saved the splendid seventeenth-century sheet of water (*left and right of the engraving*), for Elisa had commissioned the French architect Morel, who had designed the Malmaison park, to redesign the garden in the English style. The sheet of water, here illuminated for a nocturnal festivity, terminated in a splendid piece of Baroque architecture; at the far end of the balustrade we recognize the two seated statues symbolizing the two great rivers of Tuscany, the Arno and the Serchio.

Personages of the Commedia dell'Arte—Columbine in her hoop dress, Pantaloon in his simar, Pulcinella and her hump—parade on the stage of the verdant theater, one of the handsomest created in Italy (*opposite right*). The eighteenth-century statues are of terracotta. Perfectly trimmed box trees imitate the supports of a decoration, limiting the stage and the tiers in a semicircle reserved for the spectators. The theater itself is fronted by a "foyer" (*above*) reached by a rustically embossed stone porch; a few steps paved with pebbles lead to a terrace adorned with a basin and vases, then a second flight of steps rises toward the room.

# *Villa Mansi*

Segromigno

Standing in the midst of a romantic park laid out during the first half of the nineteenth century, the villa, despite its perfect stylistic cohesion, is the result of three different construction campaigns. The original building dates from the sixteenth century. In 1634-1636 the architect Muzio Oddi set flat against the façade a loggia (*left and above*) framed by two slightly emerging pavilions and surmounted by another loggia. The sculpture, including statues of Minerva, Pan, Venus and Apollo arranged in the space between the columns and the medallions representing the Four Seasons suspended from lion snouts between the arcades, also dates from the period. Finally in 1742 Fra Giovanni Francesco Giusti replaced the upper loggia by a story, topped the pavilions with balustrades and statues, and placed busts and broken pediments above the windows, giving the villa a sumptuously Baroque character, which it has since retained without change.

The engraving (*below*) gives a fair idea of the garden laid out by Filippo Juvara in 1732—a garden which, following a common custom in Italy, did not lie facing the villa but rather on the right of a large central flowerbed planted simply with grass. Enclosed by hedges, the garden, reached by means of a grille seen in the background, was conceived on a trapezoidal plan in order to increase the impression of space by means of an artificially created perspective. The arrangement of lacelike flowerbeds, basins, rows of trimmed yew trees and orange trees in pots is in the tradition of Versailles.

The transformation of the villa by Fra Giovanni Francesco Giusti in 1742 involved several projects. One of these was a plan to build a second loggia identical to that of the noble story, but instead an upper story was ultimately added (*right*).

Emerging from grinning masks, the water from the cascades flows into successive basins in that part of the park known as the "bosco" (*left*). Below the slope, an enclosure of trimmed box trees is adorned with a huge octagonal basin (*opposite right*) connected by an avenue to another basin surrounded by balustrades which we see in the background. Similar to other parts of the park, the "bosco" was laid out from the design by Juvara; an eighteenth-century engraving (*below*) shows the original plan which was modified in the nineteenth century. The octagonal basin, however, has preserved its decoration of trimmed box trees and statues almost intact.

# *Pitti Palace*

Florence

"I doubt whether there exists a more monumental palace in Europe," the French historian Hippolyte Taine wrote in his *Voyage en Italie*. "I have seen none to leave such a grandiose and simple impression... What is truly unique, and takes to the extreme the severe grandiose quality of the edifice, is the enormous materials with which it has been built... Scarcely roughed out and blackish, they retain their original barbarism. Such would be a mountain torn from its base, taken apart into courses and piled on a new site by gigantic hands."

Despite its architectural unity, the palace acquired its actual form only by successive stages. Undertaken about 1440 from the design by Brunelleschi for the banker Lucca Pitti, for whom the palace is named, it originally had seven windows on the façade on the first and second stories. Interrupted in 1466, construction was not resumed until 1549 when Eleonora of Toledo acquired the palace. Under the direction of Parigi, the façade was then extended on each side by three rows of windows in 1620 and later in the century extended again by two low wings. Finally, at the close of the eighteenth century, two low wings at right angles (not shown in the engraving above which was made prior to their erection) framed the cour d'honneur.

The reverse façade facing the gardens (*left*) consists of three main structures in the form of a horseshoe around an inner courtyard. It was erected from 1560 to 1577 by Bartolomeo Ammanati who skillfully harmonized his design with Brunelleschi's work, repeating in particular the rustic embossed coursework of the entrance façade. It is decorated with three rows of pilasters and engaged columns, Doric, Ionic and Corinthian. Salomon de Brosse took his inspiration from this elevation when he built the Luxembourg Palace for Marie de' Medici. The handsome fountain known as the "Artichoke," (*below*) overlooking the lower courtyard, is by Tadda. The Boboli Gardens, (*right*) which were laid out by Il Tribolo in 1549 and were subsequently enlarged and modified by Ammanati and Bernardo Buontalenti, contain an amphitheater adorned in the early seventeenth century by stone tiers; it was often the scene of grand ducal festivities. The perspective is continued by terraces and terminates in a huge, calm basin.

An avenue bordered by statues and known as the "Vittolone" (*below*) leads among the oaks and cypresses to the "Isolotto" or islet (*right*) created by Parigi in the early seventeenth century. In the center of a circular basin on a raised strip of grounds stands Giovanni da Bologna's statue of Oceanus with the symbolic figures of the Nile, the Ganges and the Euphrates at his feet. In its conception the ensemble was doubtless inspired by the "maritime theater" of the villa of Hadrian at Tivoli; but here the islet is a real garden with laurel trees blossoming in large terracotta pots and, unlike the case at Tivoli, it does not include a small villa.

Emerging from the formless mass of rocks, in the grotto situated in the gardens, Michelangelo's *Captives* seem to make an effort to free themselves from the material which fetters them. Originally destined for the tomb of Julius II, the original statues acquired by the Medici are now in the Academia at Florence; these are merely copies. According to a guidebook dating from the sixteenth century, the decoration of the grotto by Buontalenti in 1583 recalls the myth related by Ovid of Pyrrha and Deucalion, the only couple to escape from the Deluge. The goddess Themis orders them to cast behind their shoulders stones which will be transformed into human beings. "These stones began to lose their harshness and rigidity, and after a little, grew soft. Then, once softened, they acquired a definite shape. When they had grown in size, and developed a tenderer nature, a certain likeness to a human form could be seen, though it was still not clear." This passage from the *Metamorphoses* applies perfectly to the statues arranged in the rocaille of the grotto, but it is less suited to the rest of the decoration. The uppermost section of the walls and the ceiling are decorated with landscapes by Bernardino Poccetti, including frolicking goats, bears, leopards, monkeys and birds. At the far end of the grotto are figures of Paris and Helen sculptured by da Rossi.

# *Ducal Palace*

Urbino

In the words of Dante, "Proud Urbino, golden city," is dominated by the Ducal Palace, a huge, unfinished construction which was undertaken by Federigo Montefeltro. However, the palace as we see it today is for the most part the work of the architect Luciano da Laurana of Dalmatia. In 1468 Federigo commissioned Laurana, "that man," in his own words, "more skillful in the art of architecture based on arithmetic and geometry than any other man in Tuscany, this fertile land of architects, to build in our city of Urbino a residence in every respect worthy of our predecessors and ourselves." Laurana left in 1472 and was replaced by his chief assistant, the Sienese Francesco di Giorgio Martini. The façade facing the valley (*left*) follows the contour of the hill on which the palace is built. It is linked on the left with the cathedral, which was rebuilt in the eighteenth century. The section adjacent to the cathedral is the "castellare," an old small Montefeltro fortress encased in the new construction. The façade is marked in its center by a projecting main building flanked by two round towers crowned by pinnacles and having superimposed loggias. Hanging gardens have been laid out in the angles formed by the wings. In the sixteenth century a story unfortunately was added to the palace, so that it lacks its original crenels which were replaced by a tiled roof.

In 1466, obviously inspired by Petrarch's *Triumphs*, Piero della Francesca painted the triumph of Battista Sforza, second wife of Federigo Montefeltro; she is portrayed seated in a chariot drawn by unicorns, symbols of the countess —and future Duchess—of Urbino and surrounded by various allegorical figures, especially Charity and his pelican and Religion with his cross and eucharistic host. An impressive Umbrian landscape stretching into a hazy distance serves as background for the scene on the reverse side of a portrait of the countess, now in the Uffizi, as well as the portrait of Federigo. The latter had invited Piero della Francesca to his court and it has been said that the painter influenced Laurana in designing the palace.

The façade facing the square (*below*), seen here from the flight of steps leading to the cathedral, consists of a very long main building, followed by a wing at right angles extended by another wing attached to the first also at right angles. The principal building has, on the first story, small arched windows in the early Renaissance style, while the wings have huge bays framed by pilasters and surmounted by a lintel; the ground story is of embossed stonework. A portal leads to the inner courtyard (*right*), one of the finest architectural achievements of the Quattrocento; an arcaded gallery, supported by Corinthian columns, encloses it on four sides and supports a story adorned by pilasters. The brick and stone construction strongly emphasizes the sober design, the perfection of the outline and the purity of the proportions. The recessed upper story added in the sixteenth century unfortunately has slightly changed the original design. Running along the friezes of the ground and first floors is a long Latin inscription praising the virtues of Federigo Montefeltro, probably engraved by order of his son Guidobaldo.

MONTISFERETRI · ACDVRANTIS · COMES
DEPVGNAVIT · SEXTES · SIGNA · CONTV

The "studiolo" of Federigo Montefeltro (*opposite left*) is enclosed by armoires entirely decorated with *trompe-l'œil* marquetry representing personages in niches, landscapes and still lifes of books and musical instruments. The ruler himself is portrayed full length, in a curtain opening, not in armor but in the long robe of a humanist. Botticelli and other artists made the marquetry models which were executed under the direction of Baccio Pontelli about 1476 (the date is indicated in the ceiling of the room). Above the wooden facing there was originally an entire series of portraits of famous men—a theme dear to the Renaissance—executed by Pedro Berruguete, an artist of Spanish origin. Removed in the sixteenth century some of these portraits can be seen in another room of the palace and still others are in the Louvre.

Executed in marquetry with extraordinary precision, a figure of Pallas adorns the door leading from the Room of the Angels to the throne room (*right*). The design was furnished by Botticelli, who was also responsible for the matching figure of Apollo on the other door. The throne room—the largest one in the palace—has an outstandingly noble vault supported by rich capitals and adorned with medallions with the initials "FC"—Federicus Comes—or Federigo Montefeltro before he assumed the ducal crown. At the far end of the room the lion of Venice in low relief is a reminder that the duke was a captain of the Republic of Venice. The tapestry, part of a series with the coat-of-arms of Mazarin, for whom it was executed in the sixteenth century, represents *The Acts of the Apostles* from a drawing by Raphael.

# Latium

*Between the Tyrrhenian Sea and the Apennines, from the Tuscan Maremma to the Gulf of Gaeta, Latium, the birthplace of Roman civilization, runs along a sandy coast, whose ancient ports are almost entirely silted up. At the foot of its historic seven hills, Rome offers its forums and monuments, its basilicas, palaces and fountains celebrated by the composer Ottorino Respighi. Once the capital of an empire ranging from the Atlantic to the Euphrates, the capital of the Pontifical States until 1870, the capital of Christianity, the Eternal City is the richest museum in the world. To the east and north lie the huge, melancholic areas of the Roman countryside, its meadows crossed by aqueducts. Beyond, on the shaded hills, studded with vineyards and olive groves, rise the sumptuous villas erected by princes and prelates as security against summer fever in Rome.*

## Rome *Palazzo Doria Pamphili*

It was in the salons of the Palazzo Doria Pamphili that Handel's fine cantata "Il trionfo del tempo e del desinganno" was performed for the first time in 1707. The author of the lyrics was none other than Cardinal Benedetto Pamphili. The work enjoyed great success and particularly pleased Handel himself who had it performed again—with modifications—three times in London, first in Italian entitled "Il trionfo del tempo e della verita" in 1737 and again in 1739, then in its English adaptation "The Triumph of Time and Truth" in 1757, two years before his death.

The Palazzo Doria Pamphili was originally a palace (now replaced by subsequent constructions) erected in the first half of the fifteenth century by Cardinal Niccolò Acciapacci. It was next acquired by the Hungarian cardinal Zech, than by Cardinal Fazio Santoro. The latter completely remodelled the edifice, whose magnificence attracted the attention of Julius II. After expressing a desire to visit it, the Pope graciously admired the apartments but on departing stated that such luxury seemed to him more appropriate to a duke than to a cardinal. Intermediaries took it upon themselves to repeat the Pontiff's words to the unfortunate cardinal, who found himself obliged to offer his palace to Francesco Maria, Duke of Urbino and nephew of Julius II. According to tradition, he died of grief the following year.

The Duke of Urbino erected the portico of the inner courtyard probably from a design by Donato Bramante. In 1601 the edifice was acquired by Cardinal Pietro Aldobrandini, nephew of Clement VIII. In 1647 the marriage of Donna Olimpia Aldobrandini, Princess of Rossano, and Camillo Pamphili resulted in the acquisition of the palace by the latter's family.

Natives of Gubbio, the ancient and noble House of Pamphili had settled in Rome at the close of the fifteenth century when Antonio Pamphili responded to the appeal of Sixtus IV. Named a cardinal in 1629, Giambattista Pamphili was elected to the papacy in 1644 as Innocent X. He began his reign by prosecuting the "cardinal-nephews" of Pope Urban VIII, Francesco and Antonio Barberini, for misappropriation of funds. When they sought refuge in France, he issued a Bull in 1645 ordering the confiscation of the possessions of those cardinals not residing in the Papal States. This measure irritated Mazarin—long a friend and associate of the Barberini—who threatened Avignon, then an archepiscopal see, so that Innocent X had to yield.

Mazarin's retaliatory act displeased

*Andrea Doria*

the Pope's sister-in-law, Donna Olimpia Maidalchini, widow of his brother Pamphilo Pamphili. She expected her son Camillo to profit by the tradition of nepotism solidly established at the Papal court and was determined to advance his career without delay. An energetic woman, Olimpia had Camillo named "cardinal-nephew." (It was for her, by the way, that the Pope commissioned Pietro da Cortona to enlarge and redecorate modest Pamphili palace in Piazza Navona, and at the same time, alongside the palace he piously erected the church of Sant' Agnese and the adjacent collegiate to which he left his library.)

Camillo, however, dashed his mother's hopes by ridding himself of the cardinal's hat as early as 1647 in order to marry the Princess of Rossano, Donna Olimpia Aldobrandini, who was the widow of Paolo Borghese and mother of his son and daughter. Though previously wed, she presented one of the finest marriage possibilities in all Rome, for her uncle, Cardinal Ippolito Aldobrandini, who had died in 1638, had willed all of his possessions to the second son she might one day bear, the eldest obviously being in line to become the Borghese heir. Thus the son Camillo could expect of this marriage was destined to inherit the Aldobrandini fortune.

For their residence Camillo and Olimpia chose not the Pamphili palace in Piazza Navona—where they dreaded the proximity of the dangerous Donna Olimpia Maidalchini—but rather the present Palazzo Doria Pamphili, which was part of Cardinal Ippolito Aldobrandini's inheritance. A lover of the arts, Camillo began by commissioning important work which considerably increased the size of the edifice. In 1659 he purchased from the Jesuits a section of the terrain on which had stood the Palazzo Salviati, which they had acquired and demolished in order to enlarge their Collegio Romano. He selected the architect Antonio del Grande to build a main building which was finished in 1661. After his death in 1666 his widow, respecting the original design, extended the edifice by a perpendicular wing closing the Piazza del Collegio Romano toward the church of Santa Maria in Via Lata.

Camillo's patronage was an active and intelligent one. Thanks to him the Palazzo Doria Pamphili contained a remarkable collection of art, part of which can still be seen in the palace. Among the paintings acquired or commissioned by him are four major canvases by Caravaggio: *The Rest During the Flight to Egypt, Mary Magdalene, Saint John the Baptist* (Galleria Doria Pamphili) and *The Fortune Teller*; the latter was offered by the prince to Louis XIV and is now in the Louvre.

*Giannettino Doria*

Claude Lorrain's *Liber Veritatis* contains several sketches with the words "for Prince Pamphili." The double portrait by Raphael was part of the Aldobrandini inheritance. In addition to embellishment of the palace, Camillo finished the church of Sant' Agnese in Piazza Navona and commissioned Pietro da Cortona to design the façade of the small church of Santa Maria in Villa Lata, close to his residence.

Camillo had two sons. The elder, born in 1651, had been named Giambattista in honor of his grand uncle Innocent X. The Pope had then instituted the right of primogeniture in the Pamphili family, Giambattista becoming the beneficiary after his father's death. A special clause obliged the youngest members of the family to perpetuate the name of the Aldobrandini. In 1653 a second son was born—named Benedetto, he was destined to enter the Church. Neither Camillo nor his children cared to reside in the Pamphili Palace in Piazza Navona, preferring the present Palazzo Doria Pamphili. After the death of their father, Giambattista and Benedetto came to an agreement in 1684 to settle the rather complex business of dividing the Pamphili and Aldobrandini possessions. As a result of the agreement, Benedetto was to enjoy full use of the entire wing of the palace facing the Collegio Romano.

Giambattista failed to inherit his father's artistic taste. In his *Nouveau Voyage d'Italie* (1702), Misson wrote: "The Jesuits asked the prince to enter their Company and were indignant about the nudity of the statues. The minor prince had plaster shirts placed on every marmorean figure, man, woman and child, to the great distress of painters, sculptors and art lovers. Everything was hammered or plastered without pity except a small *Bacchus* which escaped, no one knows how, from this Massacre of Saint Bartholomew.... It happened that the prince changed his mind and preferred the company of a princess to that of the Jesuits. He then had all this ridiculous plaster work removed... but unfortunately, in order for the cement to hold, the plasterers had overscraped the marble with the result that most of the works remained badly damaged."

Benedetto was another man entirely. No sooner was he born than he was placed in a splendid bronze-gilt cradle made by Bernini, a gift of his grandmother Donna Olimpia Maidalchini. On her death in 1657, Benedetto received her entire fortune, paintings, furniture, estates and the enormous sum of two million écus which enabled the young man, who was to be named a cardinal at the age of twenty-eight, to become one of the greatest art patrons of his day.

Extremely fond of music, he wrote numerous lyrics for oratorios and cantatas not only by such composers as Handel, as mentioned previously, but also by Alessandro Scarlatti and Arcangelo Corelli, the latter having been for a while his choir master. In the part of the palace he occupied he ordered the construction of a small theater which was inaugurated in 1684 in the presence of Christina of Sweden. Certain carnival comedies presented here even aroused the anger of Innocent XII. He arranged for his apartments to be richly decorated, acquired during the course of his long life—he died in 1730—more than eleven hundred paintings, and equipped the private chapel on the first floor of the palace with a secret passage connecting it with the church of Santa Maria in Via Lata.

From 1731 to 1734 Giambattista's son built the façade of the palace overlooking the Corso, the work of Gabriele Valvassori, who also changed the inner courtyard by closing the arcades of the first story. Six years later, in 1743, Amali erected the façade overlooking Via del Plebiscito. The Pamphili family died out shortly afterward, in 1760. The palace was then inherited by the Doria Pamphili, descendants of Anna Pamphili, Giambattista's and Benedetto's sister, who had married Andrea Doria of Genoa. It is this relationship to the great admiral that explains the presence in the palace of the portraits of Andrea Doria by Sebastiano del Piombo and of Giannettino Doria by Bronzino.

The Palazzo Doria Pamphili underwent few modifications. A ballroom, however, was created in the nineteenth century. During the same period the princely collections were enriched by a splendid *Pietà* by Hans Memling, a "tondo" by Filippo Lippi and two works by Lorenzo Lotto and Il Pesellino. This taste for Primitives was rather exceptional then in Italy and the Doria Pamphili princes had probably acquired it in England, thanks to the great aristocratic collectors whom they came to know through marriages to English noblewomen.

The Palazzo Doria Pamphili is now the property of Donna Orietta and Don Frank Doria Pamphili Pogson.

## Frascati *Villa Aldobrandini*

"After making Ferrara once again obedient to the Holy See and bringing fresh peace to the Christian Republic, Cardinal Aldobrandini, nephew of Clement VIII, erected this villa, arranging for water to flow here from Monte Algido, in order to withdraw to an appropriate retreat from his urban preoccupations." This inscription, engraved in majestic Roman capitals in imitation of those on the column of Trajan, runs along the fifty-four foot frieze of the semicircle which frames the nymphaeum in the gardens of the Villa Aldobrandini. The text could be misleading, for the "reconquest of Ferrara" was anything but warlike in character. The cardinal was skillful enough to settle peacefully the knotty problem of the succession of Alfonso II d'Este, who had died in 1597, leaving as sole heir his cousin Cesare, son of a bastard of Alfonso I and Laura da Dianti. Using Cesare's illegitimacy as a pretext, the Pope claimed possession of Ferrara as a papal fief and gathered a powerful army led by his nephew, Cardinal Pietro Aldobrandini, which marched on Ferrara. Finding himself unable to withstand an attack, Cesare d'Este delegated his cousin, Lucrezia d'Este, Duchess of Urbino, to negotiate with a representative of Clement VIII for some kind of agreement which took place at Faenza. According to the terms of the Faenza Convention of 1598, he finally abandoned Ferrara but was allowed to retain Modena and Reggio.

In addition to the diplomatic success of this enterprise, Cardinal Aldobrandini gained more personal advantage from his discussions with Lucrezia d'Este. The Duchess of Urbino had fallen out with her husband, Francesco Maria della Rovere, who was much younger and had left her childless. Although she lived at Ferrara on apparently good terms with his family, it was a rankling fact that her brother Alfonso II had despoiled most of the paternal inheritance for the benefit of his successor, Cesare. The latter, moreover, had informed Alfonso II of Lucrezia's liaison with Marquis Ercole Contrari, and as a result the duke had him assassinated. The first discussion between the cardinal and the Duchess of Urbino took place on December 28, 1597. On the following January 13 the Faenza Convention was signed. The duchess died on February 12. In her will dated February 4, she left her entire fortune, a considerable sum, to the cardinal.

The cardinal (1570/1573-1621) belonged to an old Florentine family who were driven from the city by the Medici in 1553 and settled in Rome. His father was consistorial advocate. It was his uncle who established the family fortune by becoming Pope in 1592 as Clement VIII. Named cardinal in 1593, Pietro Aldobrandini was also appointed General Superintendant of Affairs of State. After showing proof of his skill in the Ferraran succession, in 1601 he negotiated between Henri IV and Charles Emmanuel of Savoy the peace which gave France Gex, Valromey and Bugey. An anonymous text of the time described him as "of simple character, impulsive, easy, officious and amicable with his friends."

The death of his uncle in 1605 marked the beginning of a period of vicissitudes for the Cardinal. Relentlessly opposed to the Aldobrandini, the new Pope Paul V (Camillo Borghese) dismissed him as vice-legate of Ferrara and he was wise enough to withdraw to his archbishop's palace at Ravenna. He spent some time at the court of Charles Emmanuel of Savoy, then finally, in 1610, he was authorized to reintegrate the Villa Aldobrandini where he was placed under "watchful residence." It is easy to understand his eagerness to join the conclave following the death of Paul V. Unfortunately, however, he was destined to die the very day Gregory XV was elected Pope, February 10, 1621.

*The "Stanza di Apollo" at Frascati*

The site of the present villa belonged to Monsignore Capranica, whose property, overloaded with debts, was seized by the Apostolic Chamber in 1596. Two years later Clement VIII offered the estate to his nephew.

Cardinal Aldobrandini at once undertook the construction of the villa and the gardens. The design was commissioned from Giacomo della Porta who directed the work until his death in 1602; Carlo Maderna and Domenico Fontana finished the edifice. Numerous painters and sculptors, including the French artist Jacques Sarazin, participated in the decoration of the salons and of the park. The villa was practically finished in the autumn of 1603 when the Pope came to stay here; he returned the following year and a splendid horserace was organized in his honor. The Pope enjoyed himself at Frascati according to a contemporary, who wrote: "Since the day before yesterday His Holiness had decided to go today to St. Peter's, but after stepping down into the garden, the fancy took him to sprinkle a new French gardener, rather amusing and even somewhat comical. His Holiness was so delighted with his pranks that their discussion continued, the moment of setting out on the journey had passed and nothing else was done that day." Of another occasion he wrote: "The Pope was in an excellent mood and wanting to enjoy himself a bit and seeing us in the antechamber, he rang, then hid himself, and on entering we failed to find him, creating much laughter."

The cardinal died in 1621 and all his possessions went to his sister Olimpia who had married a distant Aldobrandini cousin in Florence. Of the twelve children born of this union, including six sons, only two survived, Cardinal Ippolito Aldobrandini and Gian Giorgio.

The latter left only a daughter named Olimpia who inherited the wealth not only of her father but also of her uncle Cardinal Ippolito. In accordance with the terms of the testamentary arrangement between her father and uncle, as well as a trust that was made as long ago as 1611, Olimpia's second son was eventually to inherit the Aldobrandini possessions and take the family name and coat-of-arms.

Olimpia married Paolo Borghese,

then finding herself a widow in 1646, she married Camillo Pamphili. On her death in 1681 disputes arose among the children she had had of both marriages. Innocent XI then entrusted Cardinal del Luca to settle the succession. Despite the trust of 1611, the Villa Aldobrandini was given to Prince Giovan Battista Pamphili.

The latter's son Camillo died childless, leaving all his possessions to his brother Cardinal Girolamo Pamphili. When the cardinal died in 1760 his possessions, including the Villa Aldobrandini, were seized by the Apostolic Chamber which was appointed to settle his succession. One part, including the Villa Aldobrandini, was attributed to Paolo Borghese. He was succeeded by the Borghese princes, but they resided at the villa only for a short time. In the early nineteenth century Francesco Borghese, brother of Camillo and brother-in-law of Pauline Bonaparte, once again took the title of Prince Aldobrandini. His great-grandson Prince Clemente Aldobrandini is the present owner of the villa which, badly damaged by bombardment in 1943, was painstakingly restored between 1950 and 1960.

## Rome *Palazzo Farnese*

A member of a proud and noble family, possessing fine estates in the environs of Bolsena, Capodimonte, Marta and Isola Farnese, Alessandro Farnese, the future Pope Paul III, saw his career take a sudden ascendant swing when his sister, Julia Farnese, aroused a devouring passion in the heart of Alexander VI. Although he was then sixty-two years old, the Pope was deeply in love, and in November, 1493, Julia appeared at the pontifical court as the declared favorite. Married to the young Orsino Orsini, she discovered a very clever ally in her mother-in-law, Adrianna Orsini, who, determined to take the greatest advantage for herself and her son, was able to make others see reason in the outrageous affair.

Alessandro Farnese was named cardinal—"skirt cardinal" as Pasquin ironically scoffed—and was provided with numerous and fruitful ecclesiastical benefits. His favor lasted during the entire reign of Alexander VI despite a rather bitter quarrel between the Pope and Orsino Orsini in which he became involved. After taking refuge in his Castle of Bassanello, Orsini forbade Julia, who was then residing with her brother at the Farnese domain in Capodimonte, to rejoin the papal court as demanded by the Pope under threat of excommunication. Despite the Pope's insistence and threats, Julia claimed that she could not obey this order without her husband's consent. More enamored than ever, the Pope was furious and tried to bring pressure on Alessandro Farnese. "It would be a blight to my honor," the cardinal replied with dignity, "to yield to such a grave fault which for such an obvious motive would lead to a rupture with Orsini." After much wrangling, however, everything was settled as the Pope desired: Orsini yielded and was richly rewarded, Alexander VI found Julia again and the cardinal received an even more liberal share of papal favor.

He retained this favor during the pontificates that followed. In addition, his niece Laura, Julia's daughter, married one of Pope Julius II's nephews. He legitimized the children he had sired by Girolama Ruffini, recorded in history as the "beautiful unknown woman." Now that he had acknowledged his paternity, he thought of his children's future. To assure for his descendants and for himself a dwelling worthy of his glory, he undertook the construction of the Palazzo Farnese about 1514. Work was entrusted to Antonio da Sangallo, then to Michelangelo, but remained unfinished at the time of his death in 1549. After he had been elected Pope in 1534, taking the name Paul III, he began to build up a notable art collection in the palace and ordered systematic excavations for buried art treasures to be undertaken in Rome. As a result of these activities, in 1540 such famous statues as the Farnese Bull and Hercules were discovered in the Baths of Caracalla.

The interest shown by Paul III in his family—he had presented his son Pier Luigi with the duchies of Parma

*Elisabeth Farnese*

and of Piacenza which had been acquired by the Papacy—did not prevent him from being actively interested in the Church, convoking the Council of Trent by the Bull of 1536 and in 1540 approving the institution of the Jesuits. The assassination of Pier Luigi and the betrayal of his eldest grandson Ottavio who, married to Margaret of Austria, natural daughter of Charles V, had sided with his father-in-law against him are said to have hastened his death.

It was his second grandson and namesake, Cardinal Alessandro Farnese, who inherited the palace which was finished by Giacomo della Porta in 1589. In his will the cardinal specified that the works of art and paintings which were in the palace in no way must be dispersed or taken from Rome. Cardinal Odoardo Farnese, grandnephew of Cardinal Alessandro and his heir, had the grand gallery decorated by the Carracci from 1597 to 1603. On the death of Odoardo the palace was acquired by his brother Duke Ranuccio. Used as the Roman residence for the sovereigns of Parma, it was only occupied at irregular intervals.

After her arrival in Rome, where she was greeted at the city gates by Alexander VII beneath a canopy specially designed by Bernini, Christina of Sweden spent several months at the palace as a guest of the Duke of Parma. Entrusted by the duke to act as *major domo* during the queen's stay, Marquis

Giandemaria bitterly complained that the queen's servants had no scruples about burning the precious wall tapestries to obtain their gold or ransacking the furniture.

In 1727, on the death of Duke Francesco, the last male representative of the House of Parma, his niece and daughter-in-law (he had married her mother, his brother's widow), Elizabeth, Queen of Spain, inherited all the Farnese possessions. Elizabeth's son, Charles, Duke of Parma in 1731, then King of Naples in 1736 (later Charles III of Spain), removed the collections of art from the Palazzo Farnese and had them transported to Naples. They are now kept in that city's museums.

The palace was thereafter practically abandoned until "the last King of Naples," Francisco II of Bourbon and the Two Sicilies, came to reside here in 1863. Driven from his estates two years previously, the king had been the guest of Pius IX at the Quirinal after his arrival in Rome. Napoleon III, aware of the dangers to the security of the fledgling Italian state because of the presence of Francisco II in the Eternal City, tried to acquire the palace—for himself—and to persuade the deposed sovereign to leave Italy for Spain or even France, where he offered him the castle at Pau, former residence of Henri IV. The maneuver failed and the King of Naples settled down in the palace along with his family and entourage. The small court which he held there, made up of his last faithful followers, was not a gay one. Francisco's wife, Queen Maria Sophia of Bavaria, sister of the Empress of Austria and of the Countess of Trani (who had married the king's brother and lived at the Palazzo Farnese) scarcely got along with the Neapolitans in the court. She preferred long promenades in the Roman countryside, accompanied by her sister, to solemn court ceremonies. Although her conduct appears to have been without blemish, that of her sister was severely judged, for among other things she gave birth to a child sired by the Duke of Ripalda, Spanish ambassador to the Holy See.

In November, 1863, Pius IX came to the palace to visit Maximilian II of Bavaria, father of the queen and the Countess of Trani. In May, 1868, the palace was the scene of the wedding of the Count of Girgenti and Isabella of Bourbon, daughter of Isabella II of Spain. The following year was marked by a rapprochement between the royal couple—until then the marriage had not been consummated—and on December 29 the infant Christina was baptized at the palace in the presence of the Empress of Austria. Several months later the child died. The events of 1870 forced Francisco II and Maria Sophia to leave Rome and, definitely separated, they led lonely lives.

Since 1874 the palace has been the residency of the French ambassador at the Quirinal. It was repurchased by the Italian State in 1936 and rented back to the French government for a period of ninety-nine years.

## Rome *Palazzo Rospigliosi-Pallavicini*

The palace owes its origin to the ostentatious nephew of Pope Paul V, Cardinal Scipione Borghese, who built it early in the seventeenth century. The site chosen by the cardinal was the Montecavallo, on the ruins of the Baths of Constantine, then in the heart of the countryside. (The trend to build palaces and villas in the country was begun by Pope Gregory XIII in 1574 when he undertook the construction of the Quirinal Palace which was to remain the summer residence of the Popes until 1870.) After belonging for a short period to the Duc d'Altemps, the palace was acquired in 1621 by Cardinal Bentivoglio, Van Dyck's patron, who presided over the tribunal of the Inquisition which condemned Galileo. The cardinal commissioned the painters Giovanni di San Giovanni and Francesco Furini to execute the frescoes, which adorn the apartments on the first floor. In 1641, the year he was named cardinal, the palace changed hands again when it became the property of Mazarin, but he was never to reside here. A curious letter dated January 22, 1643, and addressed to M. de Chantelou, the friend and patron of Poussin, gave the reasons for this purchase. "The painting you sent me from my palace at Rome doubtlessly represents it handsomer than I found it. . . . It is the cherished retreat that I was meditating upon after the death of M. le cardinal-duc [Richelieu] and it is there that I had decided to seek relief from the pain caused by the loss of that great man. But the affection that he showed for me having passed the limits of his life, obliged him to beg the king on his deathbed to use me in the conduct of affairs." Thus Mazarin reserved a refuge for himself in the event he would be forced to leave France. In any case this purchase proves that he did not have to wait for his rise to power to establish the basis of the prodigious fortune which he subsequently amassed. The palace then housed the "mazarinettes" or the cardinal's nieces, especially the celebrated Maria Mancini. It also served as temporary residence for the illustrious guests of the French ambassador.

In 1704 Prince Giovanni Battista Rospigliosi and his wife, *née* Maria Camilla Pallavicini, acquired the palace to which they have left their names. A member of an old family originally from Pistoia, Giovanni Battista Rospigliosi was the nephew of Pope Clement IX. Maria Camilla belonged to one of the most important Genoese families and had inherited considerable possessions from her father and her uncle, Cardinal Lazzaro Pallavicini. After her marriage in 1670 the cardinal instituted a trust, according to which the possessions and titles of the Rospigliosi were reserved for the eldest son of this union, the youngest inheriting the possessions of the Pallavicini, being obliged to take the name with the title of Prince of Gallicano. However, as the result of the premature death or lack of male descendants of the youngest member of each generation, the contributions of the Rospigliosi-Pallavicini remained united until the mid-nineteenth century. At that time the princes Clemente Rospigliosi and Francesco Cesare Pallavicini shared the palaces and the collections. To the former fell the second floor of the palace, still owned by his descendants, and a part of the collections, which were sold in 1931 and 1932. The latter's descendants occupy the first floor which is still adorned with handsome furniture and paintings accumulated both by successive inheritances and by purchases.

During the centuries the Rospigliosi-Pallavicini proved to be brilliant patrons and lovers of art. Maria Camilla had inherited from the Pallavicini, especially from her uncle the cardinal, a fine group of seventeenth-century Flemish, Genoese, Bolognese and Roman canvases, notably a series of thirteen portraying *Christ and the Apostles*, the work of Rubens' pupils and retouched by the master, the *Portrait of Helen Fourment in Her Wedding Dress*, a *Portrait of a Man* by Van Dyck, and the *Perseus and Andromeda* by Guido Reni. The succession from Pope Clement I which fell to Giovanni Battista Rospigliosi in 1669 included not only a portrait of the deceased by Baciccia but also important paintings by Claude Lorrain—*Landscape with Shepherds, Landscape with Mercury, Aglauros and Herce*— commissioned by the Pope himself, as well as drawings by Bernini, among them the sketches for the angels holding the instruments of the Passion for the Sant' Angelo bridge. Giovanni Battista and Maria Camilla seemed to have a special taste for still lifes of flowers and fruit, often in large dimensions, many of which can still be seen in the palace apartments. Enriched by numerous purchases, their collection included seven hundred and forty canvases in 1713.

The palace itself underwent a few modifications in the eighteenth century, and its present furniture for the most part dates from this period. In the early nineteenth century Prince Giuseppe Rospigliosi-Pallavicini proved himself to be a particularly enlightened art collector, a man well ahead of the taste of his time, acquiring several impressive fifteenth-century Italian panels, notably the *Derelitta* attributed to Botticelli, the triptych of *The Transfiguration, Saint Jerome and Saint Augustine* and *The Virgin and Child* by the same painter, and an early *Madonna* by Luca Signorelli. The inheritance of Donna Maria Colonna Lante della Rovere added to the palace collection the splendid *Temple of Venus*, commissioned from Claude Lorrain by Prince Lorenzo Onofrio Colonna in 1672, and a very interesting *Brawl Among Soldiers* which has been attributed to Velasquez.

On the death of Prince Guido Pallavicini, the palace was inherited by his nephew and adopted son, Guglielmo de Pierre de Bernis de Courtavel. The prince and his wife, *née* Elvina Medici del Vascello, have devoted the greatest care to this great dwelling and its collections which have been enriched even further by several remarkable Italian Primitives, including the *Saint Nicholas of Tolentino* by Defendente Ferrari.

*Cardinal Scipione Borghese*

## Bagnaia *Villa Lante*

"This is a well embellished place belonging to Cardinal Gambrara," Montaigne wrote in his *Journal de Voyage en Italie* on the occasion of his visit to Bagnaia on September 30, 1581, "and above all so well furnished with fountains that in this respect it appears not only to equal but even to surpass Pratolino and Tivoli. . . . The same Tommaso da Siena who directed the work at Tivoli is directing the work here which is not yet finished. Thus constantly adding new inventions to ancient ones, he has given to the latter construction a great deal more art, beauty and embellishment . . . . The cardinal was not here, but as he is at heart a Frenchman, these people are kind and polite in every respect."

In the early thirteenth century the seigniory of Bagnaia had been given by the commune of Viterbo to the episcopal income of the municipality. Henceforth the bishops of Viterbo were lords of Bagnaia. At the close of the fourteenth century, Cardinal Raphael Riario, nephew of Pope Sixtus IV, enclosed the park with walls in order to maintain a game reserve. Early in the fifteenth century he built a hunting pavilion, still in existence, where he received Pope Leo X, who was very fond of hunting.

Leo X's nephew, Niccolò Ridolfi, brought water to the park by means of an aqueduct and began the work on the gardens. But it is to Cardinal Giovanni Francesco Gambrara to whom we are indebted for the work which gives Bagnaia its present aspect. Belonging to an illustrious family related to the Farnese, he was the nephew of the famous poetess Veronica Gambrara. Named Apostolic Administrator of Viterbo in 1566, he erected one of the two pavilions—the one which still bears his name—and laid out most of the gardens. Although unsupported by any document, the design of the ensemble has been attributed to Giacomo da Vignola, who was then working at the neighboring Castle of Caprarola. Indeed, the gardens of Bagnaia are obviously similar to the garden of the casino of Caprarola. Work was momentarily interrupted, it is said, at the request of Charles Borromeo who, scandalized by the enormous expenses involved, intervened with the austere Pope Pius V.

In 1587 Cardinal Alessandro Montalto, nephew of Pope Sixtus V, succeeded Cardinal Gambrara on the episcopal throne of Viterbo. He was aged seventeen and had received the red hat two years earlier. It was he who erected the second pavilion to match the first, although this added structure was foreseen in the original design.

In 1656 Pope Alexander VII granted Duke Ippolito Lante the seigniory of Bagnaia with a long lease (up to ninety-nine years). Henceforth the Lante dukes were to make the villa their summer residence for almost three centuries. (Pope Pius IX gave them the entire property in the mid-nineteenth century.) Louise-Angélique de La Trémoille, Duchess Lante, received her celebrated sister, the Princess des Ursins, at the villa in the second half of the seventeenth century. The latter, married for the second time to Flavio Orsini, Duke of Bracciano (she did not take the title of Princess des Ursins until her husband's death in 1698), was then defending the interests of Louis XIV at Rome in concert with the French ambassador, Cardinal d'Estrées. Worn out by the "violent ceremonies" of the pontifical villa and by the austerity of its Castle of Bracciano, the princess willingly visited her sister at whose residence colorful festivities were constantly being organized. "We have tried," she wrote, "to prevent the ambassador [d'Estrées] from being sorry for coming to Bagnaye . . . ." Music, comedy, rope dancers . . . . The two sisters were very close and very gay. The princess wrote to the duchess, who had only just recovered from childbirth; "You are the most pleasant person in the world, you cannot bear sad faces and you are right. Nor can I bear them. I detest melancholy people more than ever." And she added: "I am bringing with me personages and a mood not to trouble the festivity; they will all try to please you." Since the Duke of Bracciano was twenty-two years older than his wife, we can conclude that he was not among the party. But the pleasures of Bagnaia were perhaps not entirely innocent. Saint-Simon, a great friend of the Princess des Ursins, mentioned her morals and manners "in the fashion of a child's swing," adding, "her gallantry and stubbornness were her chief weakness and survived everything down to her final old age. Consequently she adorned herself in a manner no longer suitable to her and from age to age went always forward beyond her own."

Bagnaia suffered during World War II from bombardment and damage wrought by successive waves of occupying troops. Acquired by Dottore Angelo Cantoni, however, the Villa Lante has been completely restored.

## Tivoli *Villa d'Este*

Born in 1509, Ippolito d'Este was the son of Lucrezia Borgia (daughter of Pope Alexander VI) and Alfonso I, Duke of Ferrara. At the age of ten he was named archbishop of Milan and was made a cardinal at thirty. So precocious a career naturally led him to try to obtain the pontifical tiara.

*The Fountain of the Flirt at Tivoli*

His ambition was unsuccessful, however, and as a consolation Pope Julius III appointed him governor of Tivoli in 1550.

The cardinal lost no time in commissioning the Neapolitan architect Pirro Ligorio to design a villa and lay out a garden. Five years were needed merely to arrange the site. In 1555 the election of the reformist Pope Paul IV obliged the cardinal to leave Rome and retire to Ferrara, but work on the villa was resumed on the death of the Pope in 1559. The villa was decorated by an entire team of artists headed by Federigo Zucchero, Livio Agresti and Girolamo Muziano. In 1572, when the cardinal died, work stopped, although both the villa and the garden were almost finished. Montaigne, who visited Tivoli on April 3, 1581, stated: "Here we can see the famous palace and garden of the cardinal of Ferrara. It is a very handsome design but imperfect in several sections and the work is not being continued by the present cardinal." He admired the fountains and "this spouting of an infinite number of sprays controlled and hurled forth by a single spring, which can be moved from a great distance."

Cardinal Ippolito had left the villa to the cardinals of his family or, if there were none, to the College of Cardinals. His nephews, Luigi and Alessandro, thus succeeded him at Tivoli. When the latter died in 1624, the d'Este, now dukes of Modena, asked Pope Urban VIII to annul the will and give them the domain, and their request was granted. From that time on the villa was no longer inhabited and the gardens were left in a state of abandonment. During his journey to Italy, Fragonard was touched by their untended beauty and made a number of drawings. At the close of the eighteenth century, on the death of the last Duke of Modena of the House of d'Este, Tivoli passed into the hands of Ferdinand Hapsburg, husband of Maria Beatrice d'Este. In 1866 the villa was given to the Cardinal of Hohenlohe, Grand Chaplain of the Vatican, an important prelate who, on the eve of the Vatican Council, had dared express his hostility to the definition of the dogma of Pontifical Infallibility.

The Cardinal of Hohenlohe spent only a short time at Tivoli. But it was thanks to him that the villa enjoyed the presence of its most famous guest, Franz Liszt. In 1868 the cardinal had offered the pianist-composer, on whom he had conferred minor orders three years earlier, the use of a small apartment consisting of four rooms overlooking the gardens. Liszt made short visits, staying at the villa when he was in Rome before journeying on to Weimar or Budapest. He would stroll among the fountains, tossing the children small coins which his servant laid out for him for this purpose every morning. He immortalized the site in two piano compositions, *To the Cypresses of the Villa d'Este* and *The Fountains of the Villa d'Este*.

Every evening he would leave his retreat to dine in Rome, in Via del Babuino, at the home of Princess Wittgenstein who had been his patron for twenty years. The princess, whose daughter had married the nephew of the Cardinal of Hohenlohe, lived day and night in a shuttered apartment filled with flowers, palm trees and busts of Liszt, while in the salon were huge lighted candles whose number increased with time, since each commemorated a year of love. The princess passed the greater part of her time smoking enormous cigars as she wrote the eight volumes of her *Short Conversations for the Use of Society Women*, followed by the twenty-four volumes

*Franz Liszt*

of her *Inner Causes of the Outer Weakness of the Church*.

The ecclesiastical tonsure and dress of an abbé did not affect Liszt's passionate nature or diminish the fascination he held for women. Although fifty-eight, he aroused a devouring passion in the heart of one of his pupils, Countess Janina. At first Liszt tried to get out of her clutches, but the countess was an obstinate person. One fine morning she made an unexpected appearance in the small apartment of the villa, dressed as a man, her arms filled with flowers. . . . The inevitable followed. The affair almost turned out disastrously, for the countess proved cumbersome, following Liszt as far as Budapest, where she entered his room brandishing a revolver in one hand and a phial of poison in the other. Only when the woman suffered an opportune nervous breakdown was Liszt able to rid himself of her attentions.

On December 30, 1879, seven years before his death, Liszt gave one of his last concerts at the Villa d'Este for the benefit of the local inhabitants.

In 1917 the villa was confiscated from Austria as an enemy possession. It now belongs to the Italian State.

## Caprarola *Villa Farnese*

"We passed through Caprarola, the palace of Cardinal Farnese, of which much is said in Italy," Montaigne wrote in his *Journal de Voyage en Italie*. "In fact, I have seen no other in this country which bears comparison. . . . The building is very large, the rooms quite handsome and among others there is a salon. . . where various paintings represent the activities of Paul III and of the House of Farnese. The subjects are painted with such realism that those who have known them recognize at once, in their portraits, our constable [Anne de Montmorency], the queen mother (Catherine de' Medici), her children, Charles IX, Henri III, the Duc d'Alençon, the Queen of Navarre and King Francis II, the eldest of them all, as well as Henri II, Pier Strozzi and others. In the same room at both ends can be seen two busts [painted in fresco], on one side, and in the more honorable place, that of King Henri II, with an inscription below in which he is named preserver of the House of Farnese, and at the other that of Philip II, King of Spain, whose inscription reads 'for the great number of gifts received from him.' On the exterior there are also many beautiful things worthy of being seen, including a grotto from which the water, flowing artistically into a small lake, represents to the eye and ear the fall of natural rain."

The construction of the villa, which is actually an enormous palace, was begun by Cardinal Alessandro Farnese, grandson of Pope Paul III and the son of Pier Luigi Farnese, First Duke of Parma. His brother was Orazio Farnese who had married Diane de France, the legitimatized daughter of Henri II and Diane de Poitiers. He himself had been made cardinal at the age of fourteen and was given important ecclesiastical benefits, including the rich archbishopric of Avignon. Trying to forget the vices and cruelties of his father, who was assassinated in 1547, the cardinal revealed himself to be a refined humanist, a patron with very sure taste, who was richly praised by the poets of his time. Olivier de Magny, who knew him at Rome while in the service of the French ambassador, Jean d'Avanson, dedicated one of his odes to him:

*I will relate how you do not wish*
*To spend one day without a book*
*Knowing well that in that way you may*
*Live everlastingly*
*And that after the worthy toil*
*Of the important matters that you conduct*
*Reading within the thoughts of an author*
*You ease all your pain.*

The cardinal undertook the construction of the villa at Caprarola in 1550. He commissioned Giacomo da Vignola to design the edifice and arranged for the apartment of the noble story to be richly decorated in fresco by the Zucchero brothers.

On the death of Alessandro Farnese in 1589, the villa remained in the hands of the Farnese family until the line died out in 1731. It then passed by inheritance to the Bourbons of Spain and later of Naples. The cardinal's outstanding collections of art and his library were transported to Naples and the villa was abandoned. In the nineteenth century the Count of Caserta, brother of the last King of the Two Sicilies, resided here, but undertook no restoration work. The villa was recently acquired by the Italian State and is used as a summer residence by the President of the Republic.



*Plan of the Villa Farnese at Caprar*

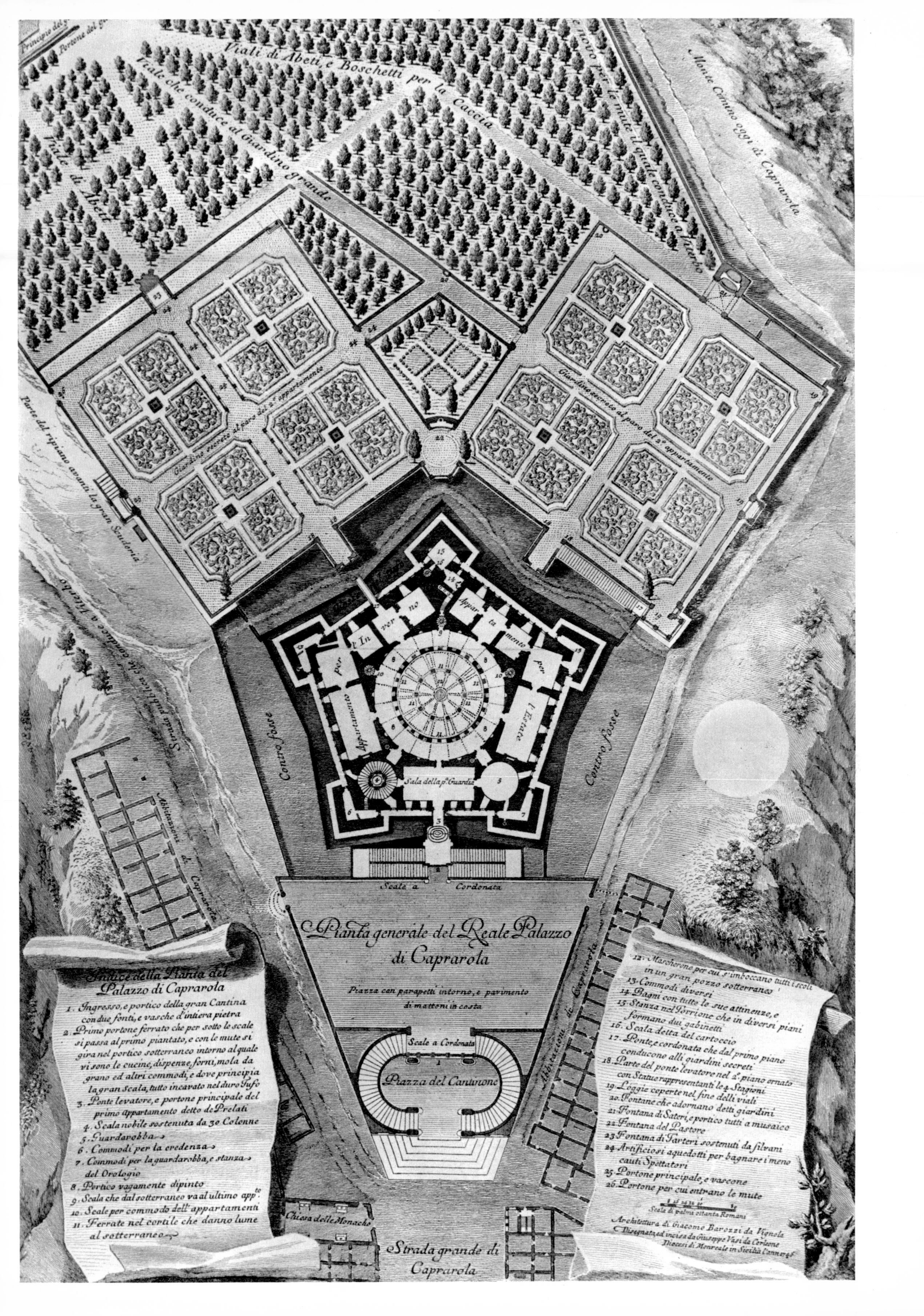
Viali di Abeti e Boschetti per la Caccia
Viale che conduce al Giardino grande
Viale di Abeti
Monte Cimino oggi di Caprarola
Giardino secreto al paro del 2.º appartamento
Contro fosse
Contro fosse
Sala della p.ª Guardia
Appartamento per l'Inverno
Appartamento per l'Estate
Abitazioni di Caprarola
Scale a Cordonata
Pianta generale del Reale Palazzo
di Caprarola
Piazza con parapetti intorno, e parimento di mattoni in costa
Scale a Cordonata
Piazza del Cantinone
Chiesa delle Monache
Strada grande di Caprarola
Palazzo di Caprarola
1. Ingresso, e portico della gran Cantina con due fonti, e vasche d'intiera pietra
2. Primo portone ferrato che per sotto le scale si passa al primo piantato, e con le mute si gira nel portico sotterraneo intorno al quale vi sono le cucine, dispenze, forni, mola da grano ed altri commodi, e dove principia la gran Scala, tutto incavato nel duro Tufo
3. Ponte levatore, e portone principale del primo appartamento detto de Prelati
4. Scala nobile sostenuta da 30 Colonne
5. Guardarobba
6. Commodi per la credenza
7. Commodi per la guardarobba, e stanza del Orologio
8. Portico vagamente dipinto
9. Scala che dal sotterraneo va al ultimo app.to
10. Scale per commodo dell'appartamenti
11. Ferrate nel cortile che danno lume al sotterraneo
12. Mascherone per cui s'imboccano tutti i scoli in un gran pozzo sotterraneo
13. Commodi diversi
14. Bagni con tutte le sue attinenze, e
15. Stanza nel Torrione che in diversi piani formano dui gabinetti
16. Scala detta del cartoccio
17. Ponte, e cordonata che dal primo piano conducono alli giardini secreti
18. Parte del ponte levatore nel 2.º piano ornato con Statue rappresentanti le 4 Stagioni
19. Loggie coperte nel fine delli viali
20. Fontane che adornano detti giardini
21. Fontana di Sateri, e portico tutti a musaico
22. Fontana del Pastore
23. Fontana di Tarteri sostenuti da silvani
24. Artificiosi aquedotti per bagnare i meno cauti Spettatori
25. Portone principale, e vascone
26. Portone per cui entrano le mute
Scala di palmi ottanta Romani
Architettura di Giacomo Barozzi da Vignola
Disegnata ed incisa da Giuseppe Vasi da Corleone
Diocesi di Monreale in Sicilia l'anno 1746

# *Palazzo Doria Pamphili*

Attributed to Donato Bramante the inner courtyard of the palace—it dates from the early sixteenth century and forms the most ancient section of the edifice (*left*)—originally had an open loggia above the gallery of the ground story. The purity of design of the noble portico was altered by subsequent remodelling. In fact, from 1731 to 1734, the architect Gabriele Valvassori filled in the arcades of the first story and replaced them with Baroque windows in order to create the galleries which encircle the courtyard on its four sides. The façade overlooking the Corso, also the work of Valvassori, was strongly criticized by his contemporaries, especially the windows on the first story with their tortuous pediments in which the bases of an attic story are inserted. Nevertheless, it is one of the finest achievements of Baroque art in Rome. We must admire the skillful way in which the architect enlivened the long flat surface by the groups of windows and portals.

"A beautiful gallery on a reception day, with its lights, filled with the rich costumes of officers, cardinals, ambassadors, ought to offer an unparalleled sight," Taine wrote in reference to the Gallery of Mirrors in the Palazzo Doria Pamphili (*below*). Indeed nowhere else can one better appreciate the splendor of pontifical and princely Rome. Built by Valvassori, the room is largely lighted by two rows of windows opening on to the Corso and also on to the inner courtyard. The vault is adorned with *trompe-l'œil* architectural motifs and with panels representing *The Fall of the Giants, The Labors of Hercules* and *The Allegories of the Four Continents* painted by Aureliano Milani. The space between the windows is adorned with mirrors elaborately framed in wood-gilt. The room retains its original furniture, wood-gilt sofas and consoles upholstered in Genoese velvet, and its collection of classical statues symmetrically aligned opposite the windows. The open door at the far end of the gallery reveals the bust of Pope Innocent X by Bernini.

The small Salon of Mirrors (*right*) owes its name to the mirrors in the angles of the room, on the doors and panels, which endlessly reflect its perspectives. The room, whose decoration dates from 1750-1760, is hung with moire with trellis frames. On the overdoors Stefano Pozzi painted children's games and in the ceiling compartments allegories of the Four Elements.

Frascati

# *Villa Aldobrandini*

Erected on the flanks of the Alban Mountains, it is the masterpiece of Giacomo della Porta who designed it in 1598 and directed the construction until his death in 1602, after which it was finished by Carlo Maderna and Domenico Fontana. On the entrance side (*above*) the huge façade is enlivened by a much higher central pavilion topped by a pediment; the terminal pavilions are adorned with a broken half-pediment which emphasizes the pyramidal aspect of the composition. The entrance portal and the wall with its oculi and vases were built during the closing years of the sixteenth century by the architect Carlo Bizzoccheri for the Pamphili, then the owners of the villa. The lily in the decoration is their emblem.

The rear façade (*right*), which is more sumptuous, has a central pavilion with porticoes and loggias in which the Baroque taste for decorative effect and disdain of classic rules are strikingly evident. The façade overlooks the splendid "water theater" (*following double page*). Set into the semicircular nympheum are five large niches flanked by statues, the work of the sculptor Ippolito Buti. Those on the ends contain Polyphemus and a centaur, while a figure of Atlas, modeled in stucco by the French artist Jacques Sarazin in 1620-1621, stands in the center niche. Atlas was originally accompanied by a statue of Hercules, helping him to support the celestial globe, an obvious allusion to Cardinal Aldobrandini aiding his uncle Pope Clement VIII.

FERRARI

AD · LEVANDAM

A delightful eighteenth-century Chinese wallpaper covers the walls of the gallery (*below*) known for this reason as the "salone cinese." In the center of the ceiling the Cavaliere d'Arpino represented the Story of Adam and Eve (1602-1603). The rich wood-gilt consoles and the cradle—used as a flower stand—as well as the chairs all date from the eighteenth century. The cornice is adorned with stars and bretessé bands representing the coat-of-arms of the Aldobrandini. The marble mosaic floor was redone in the Venetian style in the mid-nineteenth century.

The central large salon of the villa (*right*) was decorated in the first half of the eighteenth century by the painter Ammesio da Barba. *Trompe-l'œil* architectural motifs frame mythological scenes; on the overdoor is *Orpheus Holding Animals Spellbound.* The pilasters are adorned with falling flowers and masks against a background of gold and silver. The seated statue of Agrippina the Younger, Nero's mother, was discovered by Prince Aldobrandini during excavation work undertaken in his Ostia estates. This is an antique copy of the one in the Capitoline Museum in Rome.

# *Palazzo Farnese*

An impression of austere grandeur, which Taine eloquently expressed in his *Voyage en Italie*, is revealed by the façade of the palace (*right*). "Alone in the midst of a blackish square, rises the enormous palace, massive and high like a fortress. . . . Here we feel the inspiration of the great pagan age, one of tragic passions and full energy which were to be weakened and degraded by foreign domination and Catholic restoration." Construction of the palace was undertaken about 1514 for Cardinal Alessandro Farnese from the design by Antonio da Sangallo. The design, however, was modified and amplified in 1534 when the cardinal was elected Pope and took the name Paul III. On the death of Sangallo in 1546 the work was entrusted to Michelangelo from whom the Pope had also commissioned the *Last Judgment* for the Sistine Chapel and the frescoes of the Pauline Chapel, naming him prefect and architect of St. Peter's in 1547. Michelangelo designed the second story and the famous cornice above it as well as the central window, over the entrance portal, surmounted by a shield displaying the emblematic lilies of the Farnese. The palace, on which Giacomo da Vignola had also worked, was not finished until 1589 when work was completed by Giacomo della Porta, who was the architect of the rear façade. However, the balcony above the portal dates from the nineteenth century.

"One enters through a dark vestibule, full of arabesques, as solid as a postern, supported by twelve compact Doric columns of reddish granite," Taine wrote in his description of the palace. "This opens on to the splendid inner courtyard which is the edifice's masterpiece." The porch as well as the ground stories are the work of Antonio da Sangallo who probably took his inspiration from the Colosseum and the Theater of Marcellus for the courtyard elevation. The analogy was even more striking in the original design when the arcades of the first story, later filled in and made into windows, opened on to a loggia. The composition is harmonized by a twin alignment of Doric and Ionic engaged columns. The second story was designed by Michelangelo. The windows, surmounted by severely modeled pediments, are separated by an arrangement of three Corinthian pilasters which complete the classic three orders.

A watercolor engraving made in 1777 from a drawing by Francesco Panini and Ludovico Tesco (*right*) shows the Carracci Gallery still adorned with statues in niches which were later replaced by busts. The decoration of this famous gallery was executed from 1597 to 1603 on the order of Cardinal Odoardo Farnese by Annibale Carracci, assisted by Agostino and Ludovico Carracci, Domenichino and other artists of lesser renown. Inspired by Ovid and Virgil, the decorative ensemble relates the loves of the gods. In the center of the vault is *The Triumph of Bacchus and Ariadne*, while other panels arranged in the ornate frames and separated by medallions, terminal figures and *trompe-l'œil* statues, portray *Mercury Handing the Golden Apple to Paris*, various episodes in *The Legend of Galatea* and, on the overdoors in the background, *Andromeda Freed by Perseus*. The young girl holding a unicorn in her arms depicted above the entrance door is attributed to Domenichino.

In this gallery Annibale Carracci combined the influence of Raphael and Michelangelo in a composition which has an overwhelming, if not quite original, decorative effect. The gallery is a triumph of Eclecticism, so dearly cherished by the Bolognese school, which subsequently dominated all Italian and French art in the second half of the seventeenth century; Charles Le Brun and the art of Versailles were to owe much to the Carracci Gallery.

Rome

# *Palazzo Rospigliosi-Pallavicini*

In the palace garden terraced flowerbeds studded with balustrades and statues and shaded by century-old trees lead to the Casino of Aurora (*right*) erected by Giovanni Vasanzio and decorated from 1613 to 1614 with the celebrated fresco by Guido Reni to which it owes its name. The palace, an enormous edifice crowned on the angle facing the flower beds by a noble arcaded loggia, was built in the early seventeenth century by Cardinal Scipione Borghese, work being completed about 1616. The architects Flamino Poncio, Onorrio Lunghi, Giovanni Vasanzio and Carlo Maderna all contributed to its design and to that of the gardens.

One of the finest works in the important art collection of the palace is probably the triptych by Botticelli with *The Transfiguration* in the central panel and on the sides *Saint Jerome* and *Saint Augustine* (*left*). The painting belongs to the close of the artist's career and can be dated about 1500. It stands in the library on an extraordinary wood-gilt Baroque lectern with the coat-of-arms of a bishop. At the far end of the room, on a velvet-draped easel, is another gem of the collection, the *Derelitta* also attributed to Botticelli. The large armoires against the walls date from the end of the seventeenth century and contain the archives of the Rospigliosi-Pallavicini family. Around the central table are wood-gilt Roman chairs dating from the close of the eighteenth century.

Of relatively restricted dimensions, the small Gallery of Mirrors (*above*) is adorned, between the mirror panels along its arcades, with delightful gilt-stucco panels against an ivory background framed by pink marble pilasters, executed at the close of the seventeenth century. Children, foliage, falling ribbons, and arabesques on the wall panels as well as those which cover the vault, have a strong Baroque character and are evidence of a skillful understanding of the art of decoration.

Thirteen canvases portraying *Christ and the Twelve Apostles* decorate the wall covered with gold damask in the Yellow Salon (*left*). They are probably the ones mentioned by Rubens in a letter to the English ambassador dated April 28, 1618, in which the artist stated that this series was painted by his pupils and retouched by himself. They would thus be studio copies of the original work destined for the Duke of Lerma and now divided between the Prado and the National Gallery of Ottawa. The *Judgment of Paris*, which occupies the center of the far wall, is by Luca Giordano, while above the door is a *Holy Family with Saint John the Baptist* by Bassano. The wood-gilt seats upholstered with Beauvais tapestry are of Parisian origin. In the foreground is a splendid harpsichord, distinctively Roman in its Baroque exuberance, decorated with paintings on a gold background by Gaspard Poussin.

In the entrance hall (*above*), the height of which is equivalent to that of two stories, one comes across the "baldachino", a fixture in all of Rome's princely residences. It is here that cardinals left their cloaks during papal visits.

# *Villa Lante*

It was at the Villa Lante that Italian Renaissance landscape gardening produced its finest masterpiece. In fact, here the gardens almost stand by themselves, the villa is in the form of two pavilions and does not occupy the center of the composition. On the contrary, it plays almost a subsidiary role. The "quadrato" (*right*), with its basins in the center of which rises the Fountain of the Moors, attributed to Giovanni da Bologna, and its plot of box trees (redesigned in the seventeenth century), extends in front of the pavilions. A portal, modified by Cardinal Lante in 1772, once the principal entrance to the villa, dominates the old roofs of Bagnaia. The pavilion on the left (*aerial view above*) was built by Cardinal Gambrara in 1566; the one on the right was built some twenty years later for Cardinal Montalto, though it was included in the original design of the villa and gardens, whose plans have been attributed without formal proof to Giacomo da Vignola. The gardens extend in a series of terraces, lost to sight here in the greenery which scales the hill.

At command tiny sprays of water can be made to fall upon the visitor as he climbs the flight of steps connecting the "quadrato" with the first terrace adjoining one of the pavilions (*below*). Such pranks were highly appreciated in the Italian gardens of the period and devices to play them are also found in other parts of the gardens. The man responsible was Tommaso Chinucci, a hydraulic engineer born at Siena who, according to Montaigne, also worked on the Villa d'Este at Tivoli.

One of the finest "motifs" of the gardens is the so-called "water chain" (*right*) a cascade linking the third and fourth terraces which is strongly reminiscent of the gardens of the casino of the Villa Farnese at Caprarola, although here simple volutes replace dolphins. This is the reason authorities have theorized that Vignola designed the gardens.

The Fountain of the Giants (*right*), set against the third terrace, receives the water from the cascade and distributes the flow into two superimposed basins. The two bearded gods holding cornucopias are also similar to those found in the gardens of the casino of the Villa Farnese at Caprarola. Better than photographs, an ancient plan (*below*) helps us understand more clearly how Bagnaia was laid out, with its fountains and its cascades, now concealed by the greenery. On leaving the "quadrato," the visitor climbs the four terraces one after another. The first lies on the level of the noble story of the pavilions; on the second is the Fountain of the Giants set against the third terrace dominated by the water chain which rises as far as the fourth and last terrace, itself adorned with fountains and two pavilions dedicated to the Muses.

Tivoli

# *Villa d'Este*

Undertaken in 1550 from the design of the Neapolitan architect Pirro Ligorio for Cardinal Ippolito d'Este, the gardens of the villa are spread out in terraces along the Tivoli hill. They are crossed lengthwise by the avenue of one hundred fountains (*right*) with innumerable sprays of water emerging from sculptured barks, obelisks, eagles and lilies, the last two included in the arms of the Este family. In the center of the avenue, in the garden axis, a curved twin banister flight of steps (*above*) leads to the lower terrace. Sphinxes with heavy bosoms—when the water is flowing they emit two limpid sprays—mark the beginning of the steps paved with pebbles. During his journey to Italy with Abbot de Saint-Nom, Fragonard depicted the gardens in all their loveliness.

"I could not tire of the perspective which I enjoyed from the summit of the terraces," Chateaubriand wrote after his visit to the Villa d'Este (*following double page*). "Above you extend the gardens with their plane trees and cypresses. After the gardens come the remains of the house of Maecenas placed on the bank of the Anio. On the other side of the river, on the hill opposite, reigns a wood of old olive trees with the debris of the Villa of Varus." Since that date the landscape has scarcely changed. From the terrace spread out before the villa, adorned by a handsome classical tripod, we see in the distance the Sabine Mountains dominated by the peak of the Soracte.

"The music of the organs," Montaigne wrote in reference to the fountain of the same name (*left*), "which is real music and genuine organs, sounding nevertheless always the same thing, is achieved by means of the water which falls with much violence into a round, vaulted cellar and affecting the air there forces it in order to emerge to reach the organ pipes and furnish it with wind. Another water, pushing a completely indented wheel, causes the keyboard of the organ to beat in a certain order; one can also hear the sound of false trumpets. Elsewhere one hears the sound of birds. . . ." The clever arrangement was the work of the Frenchman Claude Vénard. The fountain by the sculptor Pirrin del Gaglioardo is an impressive architectural composition consisting of a central niche supported by two caryatids and crowned by a pediment dominated by the Este eagle. In the niche a small pavilion topped by a dome replaced in the seventeenth century the statue of Diana which originally stood here.

A statue representing Rome, seated, wearing a helmet and brandishing a spear (*above*), marks the entrance to that part of the park known as "Rometta." Cardinal Ippolito d'Este had reproduced here on a smaller scale some of the most famous monuments of ancient Rome, including the Pantheon, the Mausoleum of Augustus and the Capitol. These decorative models of the architectural glories of antiquity which, for the most part, have since disappeared, were used as the setting for theatrical performances.

Immortalized by Liszt, the fountains of the Villa d'Este are without doubt the finest and most famous in all Italy. They aroused the admiration of Montaigne who saw them on April 3, 1581.

The Fountain of the Dragons (*left*) by Pirro Ligorio was created in honor of Pope Gregory XIII whom Cardinal Ippolito d'Este received at Tivoli in September 1572. The dragons are patterned after those included in the arms of the Buoncompagni family to which the Pope belonged. The Fountain of the Organ (*right*), bristling with sprays and streaming with cascades, dominates the perspective of the "peschiera" (*below*). These sheets of water in the lower part of the park were originally fish ponds to supply the cardinal's table with fish on meatless days.

The central grand salon (*below and right*) of the apartments on the ground floor is decorated on one side with a fresco of special interest, for it represents the gardens of the Villa d'Este as they appeared in the sixteenth century and rather different from what they are today. (Although the series of terraces has remained, the vegetation has developed considerably, especially in the lower part originally decorated with flower beds and trellis supports.) The ceiling, which was begun by Girolamo Muziano and his pupils and was finished by Federigo Zucchero, groups the entire Olympus. The central motif is devoted to the banquet of the gods; in the voussoirs in the midst of grotesques and arabesques are medallions representing Juno, Neptune, Apollo and others as well as sacrifices offered to Diana, Apollo, Ceres and Bacchus, while in the corners we find Mars and Venus, Bacchus and Ceres, Jupiter and Juno, Mercury and Minerva framing the coat-of-arms of the Este family—an eagle surmounted by a lily—a motif repeated everywhere in the decoration of the room. One of the walls of the salon is adorned with a niche containing a fountain where we see, executed in mosaic and rocaille, a landscape with the Temple of the Sibyl at Tivoli.

# *Villa Farnese*

Caprarola

With its austere and majestic beauty, as well as because of its size, the villa is more a palace than a country residence (*left and above*). It was built in 1550 by Giacomo da Vignola for Cardinal Alessandro Farnese, who had to take into account the existence of a fortress begun earlier by Antonio da Sangallo and left unfinished, thus explaining the pentagonal design of the edifice. The villa, whose ground story is flanked on each angle by a massive bastion, stands on a sloped foundation; access is by means of ramps. The noble story, adorned in the center by a loggia, now paned, is surmounted by two stories destined for the cardinal's suite. No ornamentation affects the purity of the pilasters, the perfection of the design and the stark bossage which enliven the elevation. The circular inner courtyard is distinguished on the ground story and on the noble story by two galleries which are beautifully harmonized by Ionic columns, arcades and niches.

Mentioning the villa in his *Journal de Voyage en Italie*, Montaigne wrote: "There is a splendid salon whose ceiling (for the whole edifice is vaulted) represents a celestial globe with every figure included (*above*). This celestial globe is painted along the entire wall of the salon with every region, thus forming a complete cosmography. These very rich paintings cover the entire walls." On the ceiling, in a resplendent stucco setting, we can still see the figures of the planets and of the constellations and on the walls the maps of various continents as they were imagined at that period. This decoration, which reflected the literary taste and geographical curiosity of Cardinal Alessandro Farnese, is the work of the brothers Giovanni and Taddeo Zucchero.

The decoration of the reception rooms, also by the Zucchero, is for the most part devoted to the glorification of the Farnese family, especially to Pope Paul III, the cardinal's grandfather. In one of the rooms (*right*), framed by arabesques, are represented various episodes in the life of the Pope with appropriate comments and inscriptions in Latin. We see him portrayed on the ceiling wearing a tiara as he receives the surrender of the city of Perugia and persuades Charles V and Venice to intervene against the Turks. On the large fresco (*left*) he is arranging the Truce of Nice between Charles V and Francis I. Finally the fresco on the right commemorates the most important event during his reign, the convocation of the Council of Trent.

PAVLVS III PONTIFEX MAXIMVS
PERVSIAM POST DEFECTIONEM
AD OFFICIVM ATQVE
OBEDIENTIAM COMPELLIT
ANNO A PARTV VIRGINIS
CIↃ D XL

Harmonized in its helical ascension by a series of twin Tuscan columns, the "Scala Regia" (*right and below*) is Vignola's masterpiece and without doubt the finest staircase created during the Renaissance. It occupies the left angle of the entrance façade and leads to the grand apartments on the noble story, then to those on the upper one. In the frieze between triglyphs are the lilies of the Farnese coat-of-arms. The vault is decorated with arabesques and grotesques, while on the partition wall between niches the large landscapes by Antonio Tempesta appear as windows open to the surrounding countryside.

Delightfully relaxing after the awesome splendor of the villa, the casino standing in the gardens is at once intimate and refreshing to the spirit, at the same time reflecting the grandeur appropriate to a Prince of the Church. A fountain (*left*), framed by two bearded giants (*below*) bordered by stone dolphins holding cornucopias, flows into a cascade bordered by stone dolphins which terminates in a shell-shaped basin. On either side of the cascade—which is very similar to that of the Villa Lante at Bagnaia—two soft slopes rise between the walls supporting the terraces as far as the garden bordered by graceful canephori or basket bearers (*right*) fronting the casino, which has a loggia decorated with frescoes on the first story. The garden and the casino were finished in 1587.

# Emilia-Romagna

*The Via Aemilia, the Roman Way dating from 187 B.C., has given its name to the plain which crosses from Piacenza to Rimini. Limited by the Po, the Adriatic, the Apennines and the Trebbia Valley, Emilia south of Bologna becomes Romagna. During the Middle Ages several states shared this fertile region, with its various crops, which ends along the coast in huge lagoons now being drained. Bologna, celebrated for its campaniles and its university, conquered by Pope Julius II in 1506, was annexed to the Cisalpine Republic by Napoleon in 1796. From 1831 to 1848 the Austrians reigned with a heavy hand. Ferrara, fief of the House of Este until 1598, was to become in that year a pontifical possession; the Este had to be satisfied with Modena, which they did not give up until 1860. The destiny of Parma proved a more tormented one. Falling into papal suzerainty, the town was given in 1545 by Pope Paul III to his son Pietro Luigi Farnese. In 1727 the Spanish Bourbons, heirs of Elizabeth Farnese, became the rulers of Parma. A French possession under the Empire, the duchy did not become a possession of the Bourbons again until 1847. Finally, in 1860, it became part of the new Italy.*

## Bologna *Palazzo Montanari*

"This furious nuncio so worthy of the time of the Guise!" Such is the concise word portrait sketched by Saint-Simon of the future cardinal Pompeo Aldrovandi for whom the palace was built. Actually Aldrovandi seemed to have been a man of rather peaceful character. He was named nuncio in Spain in 1715 at a period when relations were extremely strained between Philip V and the Holy See which, in 1709, under pressure from the emperor, had recognized Archduke Charles as King of Spain. The nunciature was then closed. Aldrovandi's role was therefore to renew diplomatic relations between the two countries. On the one hand, Pope Clement XI wanted very much to obtain from Spain a fleet which he intended to use to repulse a possible attack by the Turks. On the other, Alberoni, Philip V's all-powerful minister, wanted at any cost to be named cardinal and the Pope, who had little illusion about his virtues, hesitated to grant his wish. Poor Aldrovandi found himself caught between the tree and the bark in an attempt to defend Alberoni's interests without betraying his sovereign. Despite his skill and courage, his mission failed. Alberoni obtained the cardinal's hat in 1717, but relations between Madrid and Rome remained so strained that a year later diplomatic relations were again broken off and Aldrovandi had to leave Spain. "The rupture foreseen by the nuncio occurred," Saint-Simon wrote, "and despite the wisdom of his advice, Rome and Madrid blamed him for the entire iniquity of an event which he had attempted to prevent."

Born into an aristocratic Bolognese family, Pompeo Aldrovandi (1668-1752) had been named archbishop of New Caesarea. His failure in Spain did not prevent him from following a brilliant ecclesiastical career. He was patriarch of Jerusalem, governor of Rome in 1733, cardinal the following year and legate at Ravenna. Charles de Brosses gave a capsule summary of his qualities at the time of the conclave following the death of Pope Clement XII: "Bolognese of a good family, a good mind, palpable subject." As early as 1725 Aldrovandi had undertaken the construction of his palace at Bologna, which was not finished until the day before he died in 1752. Work was directed by Francesco Angelini, who died in 1731 and was followed by Alfonso Torreggiani. The huge dimensions of the edifice seem to confirm the rumors mentioned by Saint-Simon, according to which Aldrovandi skilfully managed his affairs. At the time when he had to leave Spain, "it was said that, being in the habit of making the most of his money, he had recently taken these measures to remove from merchants the sums he had lent them at interest." Moreover, according to tradition at Bologna, when questioned on the subject of the income which he had made from his palace—partly rented as was the Italian custom—the cardinal replied: "Anyone who is afraid of the devil would gain two hundred *scudi*, anyone who is not afraid would gain a good four hundred. . . . As for me, it has brought me eight hundred *scudi*."

His heirs preserved the palace until 1857 when Count Luigi Aldrovandi sold it to Prince Alessandro Torlonia, who in 1860 gave it in turn to Signore Camillo Montanari, great grandfather of the present owner, Signore Filippo Montanari.

## Ferrara *Castello Estense*

On February 2, 1502, Lucrezia Borgia made a solemn entry into Ferrara, where she had arrived to marry Alfonso d'Este, son of the reigning Duke Ercole I. Seventy-five archers opened the procession, followed by trumpeters, gentlemen, officers and princes. The bride was preceded by over twenty Spaniards dressed in black and gold, six bishops and the diplomatic corps. Mounted on a mule she appeared beneath a canopy, wearing an opulent "camora" with its large sleeves partly covered by a cloak lined with ermine. On her neck and in her hair was a brilliant array of diamonds and rubies presented by her father-in-law. The chronicler Cagnolo left a description of the twenty-two-year-old woman: "She is medium built and rather elegant, the face a bit long, the nose quite straight. . . clear pale-blue eyes, a rather large mouth and very white teeth; her breasts are not outstanding but amply provided." Her blonde hair has been immortalized in the frescoes painted by Bernardino Pinturicchio in the Borgia apartments in the Vatican.

Lucrezia Borgia *by Pinturicchio*

The wedding festivities lasted five days. A theater to hold five thousand spectators had been arranged in the palace, where comedies by Plautus were given, between ballets and processions of allegorical chariots. Lucrezia Borgia proved particularly outstanding for her execution of Moorish dances. Pious interludes interrupted these frivolous divertisements. Among these was one where the entire court went to the bedside of a nun named Lucia, on whom there appeared, on Friday the 4th, the five wounds of the Passion. Despite these occasions the wedding, according to Lucrezia's sister-in-law, Isabella, Marquise of Mantua, was not lacking in gaiety. The gift of the King of France, an engraved "enseigne" representing Mary Magdalene, took the form of a cruel allusion to the erring ways of the young bridegroom. However, on the morning after the wedding members of the family decided not to proceed with the "matinata," the visit made to the newlyweds still lying in bed in order to tease them with more or less spicy jests.

The marriage desired by Cesare Borgia and Pope Alexander VI had been concluded under constraint. Lucrezia was merely an instrument in the hands of her brother and father who were devoured by ambition, and Duke Ercole d'Este, unwilling to displease the Pope and his son, had agreed despite his qualms. Lucrezia had a shadowed past. Her first marriage, to Giovanni Sforza, lord of Pesaro, had been annulled on the pretext of her husband's impotence. Her second husband, Alfonso of Aragon, had been assassinated, it was rumored, by order of Cesare Borgia. The young woman was also said to have had scandalous relations not only with her brother but with her father as well, and the Neapolitan poet Pontano had composed her epitaph in Latin: "Daughter, wife and sister-in-law of Alexander." It appears, however, that the chroniclers of the period had, out of malice and spite, greatly exaggerated the facts.

*Alphonso I d'Este*

Lucrezia won the love of her husband and the appreciation of her father-in-law. The most famous poets and humanists vied with one another to praise her beauty and merits. On the occasion of her marriage to Alfonso d'Este, Ariosto had composed a nuptial poem of one hundred and fifty Latin hexameters in which he described her as "pulcherrima" and—rather strangely—as "romana virgo." Baldassar Castiglione mentioned her with praise in his *Il Cortegiano*, a manual for courtiers. She inspired Bembo, poet, historiographer and cardinal, with a passion that antagonized Alfonso d'Este and resulted in a rich correspondence. Although Bembo's letters reveal his platonic tendencies, it is uncertain that his relations with Lucrezia were absolutely pure. Although the duchess later appears to have had a liaison with her brother-in-law, Francesco Gonzaga, Marquis of Mantua, such lapses were kept secret and created no scandal. Lucrezia, moreover, rewarded her husband with numerous children, the last of whom caused her death in 1519 when she was only thirty-nine. One of the most curious opinions of her is that of the French military hero Pierre Bayard, who defended Ferrara against the encroachments of Pope Julius II. "Who dares to say that neither in this period nor much earlier has there been found a more triumphant princess, for she was beautiful, good, sweet and courteous to everyone. She spoke Spanish, Greek, Italian and French somewhat, Latin very well and wrote in all these languages. It is quite certain that, however her husband was wise and brave, the said lady, by her grace, was the reason for his fine and loyal service." The Castello Estense was erected at the close of the fourteenth century by Niccolò II d'Este, a member of a family which had imposed its domination on Modena and Reggio as early as the twelfth and thirteenth centuries. Another member of the family, Obizzo d'Este, enjoyed the questionable honor of being included in Dante's *Inferno* among "the tyrants thirsty for pillage and blood."

The prisons of the castel were the scenes of tragic episodes, for it was here that Niccolò III confined and executed his young wife Parisina Malatesta and his son Ugo, who was declared guilty of having seduced her. Ferrante and Giulio d'Este, the illegitimate sons of Ercole I, were also imprisoned here for a period of seventeen years by order of their half-brother Alfonso whom they had wanted to assassinate. In fact, the latter had sided with his legitimate brother Cardinal Ippolito d'Este who, jealous of the favors granted to Giulio by Angela Borgia, had his eyes gouged out by his squire.

But life in the Castello Estense was not always so blood-stained. In the early fifteenth century, Leonello, son of Niccolò III, invited Pisanello and Alberti to his court. Borso, his brother and successor, received from the emperor the title of hereditary duke of Modena and Reggio, and from Pope Paul II that of Duke of Ferrara. But it was the reign of Ercole I that marked the beginning of the most glorious period of the Ferraran court. The duke laid out entire quarters which enlarged the city and proved to be the first examples of urban planning in the modern sense of the word. The poet Boiardo read before the court his *Roland in Love* which enjoyed enormous success at that time. Patronized by Cardinal Ippolito, Ariosto composed his *Orlando Furioso*. Duke Ercole was equally interested in the theater and on January 25, 1486, for the first time since antiquity, the Castello Estense was the scene of a performance of Plautus' comedy *Menaechmi*. Antonio Pistoia's *Panfila*—the first classic tragedy in imitation of Seneca but written in Italian—was also performed at Ferrara during Lent of 1499.

The dukes of Ferrara were the patrons of the masters of the School of Ferrara. Borso in particular had commissioned Cosimo Tura and Francesco Cossa to execute the frescoes of the Palazzo Schifanoa. Alfonso I, husband of Lucrezia Borgia and brother of Isabella d'Este, Marquis of Mantua, and of Beatrice d'Este, who married Ludovico il Moro, turned to the services of some of the greatest Venetian, Roman and Florentine artists. In 1516 he invited Titian to the Castello for the purpose of finishing, aided by his two assistants, *The Feast of the Gods* which is now in the National Gallery, Washington. About 1520 Titian executed for him the splendid *Bacchanalia*, now in the National Gallery, London. Alfonso I asked Leonardo da Vinci to paint a *Leda*, but was responsible for the unfortunate notion of melting the colossal statue of Pope Julius II (executed by Michelangelo for the door of San Pietro at Bologna) when he captured the city in 1511.

Ercole II, son of Alfonso I and Lucrezia Borgia, was the patron of Tasso when he wrote the major part of *Jerusalem Delivered* which was dedicated to the Duke. It was also at the court of Ferrara, in 1573, that *Aminta* was performed for the first time. In 1528 Ercole II had married Renée de France, daughter of Louis XII. A pupil of Lefevre d'Etaples, the duchess had received at Ferrara some of the Protestants driven out of France; Clement Marot,

*Ercole I d'Este*

who mentioned her marriage in his poems, was her secretary after the "Affaire des Placards" in 1535 and Calvin preached before her the following year. About 1540 she appears to have ceased to practice the Catholic religion. Her attitude, however, alienated her from her husband who, fearful of displeasing the Pope, drove the Protestants from his territory and appealed to Henri II. The King of France at once sent to Ferrara the Grand Inquisitor Ory who, in 1554, condemned Renée to life imprisonment. She was liberated shortly after agreeing to confess her sins and receive Holy Communion, but she soon renewed relations with the Protestants and remained in correspondence with Calvin. Her oratory, evidence of her pious meditation, still exists at the Castello Estense.

She also had less compromising friends, however, and in 1538 received at Ferrara Vittoria Colonna, Marquise of Pescara and patron of Michelangelo, and her aunt Isabella d'Este. Writing to Ercole Gonzaga, the Cardinal of Ravenna described one of their discussions. "Yesterday evening we enjoyed a very special diversion. The duke [Ercole] and I as well as the marquise [Vittoria Colonna] were having supper with your august mother [Isabella d'Este]. After the meal the marquise read five of her sonnets to us; they are so wonderful that no angel in heaven could write anything so perfect. After this reading which we infinitely enjoyed, your mother's ladies came to join us and skillfully played a few pieces on the gravicembalo."

After the death of Ercole II in 1559, Renée returned to France and settled at Montargis. Their son Alfonso succeeded his father and received Montaigne at the Castello on November 16, 1580. "Wednesday morning," Montaigne wrote, "M. d'Estissac and I went to pay our respects to the duke. He was informed of the visit and sent a lord from the court to greet us and lead us to his cabinet, where two or three others were with him. We passed through several closed rooms where several well-dressed gentlemen were standing. We were all requested to enter. He received us standing at a table and awaiting our arrival. He raised his cap as we entered and remained uncovered all the while I spoke with him. He first asked me if I understood Italian, and when I said I did, we conversed on various topics. I also saw the state barge that the duke had built for his wife—who is a very pretty woman and much too young for him."

The death of Alfonso II in 1597 marked the end of the dazzling court life at Ferrara. His marriages, first to Lucrezia de' Medici, then to Barbara of Austria and finally to Margherita Gonzaga, had all been childless. The closest heir was Cesare d'Este, son of a bastard of Alfonso I and Laura de Dianti. After the Faenza Convention of 1598, the Pope took advantage of this to lay his hands on Ferrara, leaving Cesare d'Este merely the duchies of Reggio and Modena.

*Niccolò II d'Este*

Emptied of its treasures, which were transported to Modena, the palace was used until the time of the French Revolution as the residence of the cardinal legate. It is now the property of the Italian State.

Parma

## *Rocca di Soragna*

Since at least the close of the tenth century, the domain of Soragna was a part of vast territories extending into Tuscany and Lombardy and under the control of the Obertenghi. The Obertenghi divided into several branches among whom these territories were divided during the tenth, eleventh and twelfth centuries: the House of Este, Massa, Pallavicini, Cavalcabo, Lupi di Soragna and Malaspina. In the eleventh century Soragna belonged to the Pallavicini. But in 1198 Guido Lupi, ancestor of the present Prince Meli Lupi di Soragna, already enjoyed the title of Marquis of Soragna. He was chief magistrate of Parma in 1202 and successfully settled the disagreements between his city and Piacenza over Borgo San Domenico, now Fidenza. One of his sons, Montini, whom a chronicler described as "a lion on the battlefield," contributed to the victory the Guelfs achieved at Vittoria over Emperor Frederick II, which was to mark the beginning of the decline of the Hohenstaufen. The Lupi occupied a strategically important geographical position and were among the most ardent supporters in Northern Italy of the Guelf party. During the many struggles which occurred in the region, the Rocca di Soragna was burnt down several times and rebuilt. We still find, covered by more recent buildings, the remains of crenels dating from the medieval period.

When Giberto da Corregio was tyrant of Parma, the Lupi revolted against his domination and were forced to go into exile until his fall. In 1347 Ugolotto Lupi obtained from Emperor Charles IV recognition of his title of marquis and of his right over the land of Soragna which, as freeheld land, became a fief. This recognition was a reward for adhesion to the Guelf party on the part of the Lupi, enemies of the Ghibellines, who had supported Giberto da Corregio. The tomb of Ugolotto Lupi is found in the chapel of the Rocca di Soragna.

During the rise of the Visconti to power at Milan, the Lupi possessions were seized and they had to seek refuge at Padua. Several members of the family entered the service of other powerful lords as condottieri. Bonifacio, Ugolotto's son, fought in the Florentine ranks. He founded at Florence the Bonifacio Hospital in Via Gallo and at Padua the Lupi Chapel in the basilica of St. Anthony. At the close of the fourteenth century Bonifacio and his cousin Antonio rebuilt the Rocca di Soragna. They became reconciled with the Visconti through Bonifacio Lupi's nephew and heir, Ugolotto Biancardo, famous for his talents as a warrior and a great general under Gian Galeazzo Visconti. One of Bonifacio Lupi's cousins, Simone Lupi, was chief magistrate of Padua several times and in 1374 presided over the funeral of Petrarch, who was his friend.

Francesco Lupi, Ugolotto Biancardo's son-in-law, received the heritage of several branches of his family. Since his grandson Diofebo I had no son, all his possessions, including the Rocca, were left to the son of his sister Caterina, who had married Giambattista Meli. The latter was a member of a noble Cremonese family. He encountered the utmost difficulty in receiving for his son, still a minor, the inheritance of Diofebo, whose brothers wanted to annul the will. Meli and Lupi turned to Pope Leo X to decide the issue and discovered the fate of "small sovereigns relying on the king." The Pope decided to hand the fief over to his brother Giuliano de' Medici, who in turn gave it to his wife, Philiberte of Savoy. However, the son of Giambattista Meli and Caterina Lupi, Giampaolo, who assumed the title of Marquis Meli Lupi, succeeded in regaining his land from Philiberte of Savoy for the sum of fifteen thousand gold *scudi*. In 1530 Charles V confirmed his right to bear the names of Meli and Lupi and to include the imperial eagle in his coat-of-arms. The document signed by the emperor is now kept in the family archives. However, the claimants to the inheritance did not abandon the issue until 1536 when Giampaolo regained possession of his castle.

*Prince Giampaolo Maria de Soragna*

*Princess de Soragna*

It was his descendants, however, who decorated and embellished the edifice. During the sixteenth century, under the direction of Parmigianino, Giulio Campi executed the frescoes of the room which bears his name and Baglione decorated the walls of the large entrance room with remarkable grotesques.

A tragedy marked the life of Diofebo II Meli Lupi, Giampaolo's son. His wife Cassandra was assassinated under mysterious circumstances by his brother-in-law, Count Giulio Anguissola. According to legend, the ghost of the unfortunate woman, named by the village people "Donna Cenerina" or lady of the ashes, haunts the castle, especially when a member of the family dies. Giampaolo II, son of Diofebo and Cassandra, married Isabella Pallavicino di Cortemaggiore who, in 1581, at her own expense, had Erasmo Viotti print at Parma a splendid edition of *Jerusalem Delivered*, reread and corrected by Tasso himself.

Born in 1601, Diofebo III, grandson of Giampaolo II, fortified the Rocca by order of the Duke of Parma. But it was Giampaolo Maria who more than any other left his mark on the castle. As early as 1681, after his marriage to Ottavia Rossi di San Secondo, he arranged the "noble apartment" in an exuberantly handsome style. A man of haughty and difficult character, in 1709 he obtained from the Emperor Joseph I the title of Prince of the Holy German Empire; he was later made a grandee by Philip V of Spain.

In 1735, during the War of the Polish Succession, the Rocca di Soragna was besieged by the Franco-Spanish army, Prince Meli Lupi having sided with the Imperials. After the French Revolution and the campaign in Italy, the feudal rights of the princes of Soragna were abolished. Prince Casimir I was a member of the delegation invited to Paris on the occasion of the birth of the King of Rome. After the fall of the empire, he as well as his wife were highly appreciated by Marie-Louise, ex-empress of the French and Duchess of Parma, who painted a delightful portrait of his children, now kept in the Rocca together with letters from the sovereign.

For some twenty years Prince Bonifazio Meli Lupi di Soragna, the present owner of the castle, and his wife, Princess Margherita Violetta, *née* Quaranta di Zullino, have devoted their efforts to restoring and enhancing their magnificent dwelling and to making it an important cultural center. The library, containing more than 12,000 volumes, including numerous works by the celebrated Venetian printer Aldus, has been methodically classified, as have the archives, whose most ancient document dates from 1033. Among those signed by emperors, kings and princes are letters by Prince Eugene de Savoy, Empress Maria Theresa and Marie-Louise. The prince generously receives art historians, scholars, bibliophiles, poets, philosophers and artists. In 1963 he founded the Soragna Prize which is given annually for a graphic work, drawn or engraved, selected by a jury consisting of the leading art critics in Italy. The originality and informality of the prize—a huge cheese of the region known as "grana" and an ample supply of wine—has done much to contribute to the success of the enterprise.

The oldest male member of the family now bears the title of the Prince of the Holy Empire and Prince of Soragna; other members of the family hold the titles of marquis and patrician of Venice.

# De par le Roy

A tous gouverneurs et nos Lieutenans generaux en nos provinces et armées, gouverneurs particuliers et Commandans de nos Villes, places et troupes, Et à tous autres nos officiers, Justiciers et sujets qu'il appartiendra, Salut. Nous voulons et Vous mandons très expressement que Vous ayez à laisser seurement & librement passer le Comte de Soragna retournant à Parme avec ses domestiques hardes et bagages

sans lui donner ny souffrir qu'il lui soit donné aucun empêchement, Mais au contraire toute l'ayde et assistance dont il aura besoin; le présent passeport valable pour trois mois seulement: Car tel est notre plaisir. Donné à Versailles le quatorze Janvier 1756.

Louis

Par le Roy

Rouillé

Gratis

# *Palazzo Montanari*

Majestic in size, the grand staircase of the palace is the work of Francesco Angelini, architect of the Bolognese Senate, who in 1725 undertook the construction of the edifice for the Cardinal Pompeo Aldrovandi. Ornamental vases mark the banisters with their strong balustrades. On the first floor the doors are surmounted by Baroque pediments framing coats-of-arms with their skillfully interlaced silhouette. Somber wooden doors with rather plain mouldings emerge from the walls which are painted in two tones; white for the architectural motifs and pale ochre for the backgrounds.

A grimacing satyr carrying under each arm a monster with the wings of a bat adorns the entrance gate to the palace (*left*); the bronze group is hanging from the jaws of a strange animal which appears to resemble a lion. More extraordinary still is the key opening in the form of a gorgon's head with its mouth framed by serpents.

The façade of the palace (*above*) is the work of the architect Alfonso Torreggiani who replaced Francesco Angelini when the latter died in 1731. The edifice is built of brick and stone with a design of regular panels against a brick background. The balconies, the pilasters and the pediments are also of brick, and this rigid design is enlivened by the central balcony with its twisted motif arranged above the entrance portal and the pediment.

# *Castello Estense*

In 1385, after an uprising caused by fiscal problems, Niccolò II d'Este decided to erect a fortress which would enable him to dominate Ferrara and impose his will on the populace. Construction was entrusted to the famous military engineer Bartolino Ploti. Work progressed rapidly and at the close of the fourteenth century the Castello was more or less as we see it today. Four main buildings frame a courtyard with a heavy square tower at each angle. One of these (*opposite, in the background, left*), known as the "lion tower," dates from before the castle and was once part of the Gate of the Lions in the city's ramparts. The Castello was modified in the sixteenth century after a fire in 1554 which destroyed its upper sections. The four main buildings were then raised a story under the direction of Gerolamo Carpi, and a marble balustrade replaced the original crenels above the machicolation. It was then also that the towers were crowned with pavilions adorned with pilasters and niches. Finally, in 1570, Alfonso II topped these pavilions with small lantern-turrets designed by Alberto Schiatti. The entrance pavilion (*opposite on the far left*), which fronted the bridge spanning the moats, was enlarged and modified in the seventeenth and eighteenth centuries.

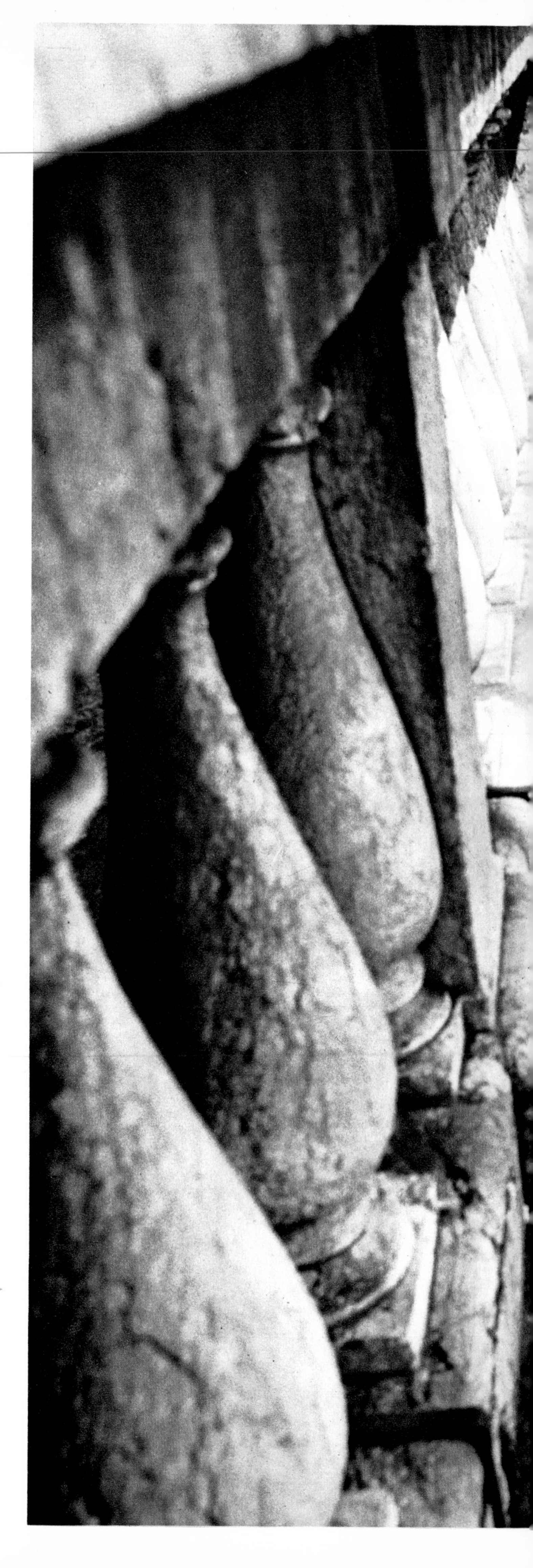

Entirely covered with slabs of colored marble inserted in high mouldings, the oratory (*above*) is that of Renée of France, daughter of Louis XII and wife of Ercole II d'Este. According to tradition the duchess insisted on this marble facing in order to avoid hanging "pictures" which were not permitted by the Protestant religion to which she was partial. The oratory was the scene of pious meditation by Marot and Calvin whom Renée welcomed at Ferrara in 1535 and 1536 with numerous other Huguenots.

A haven of grace and solitary peace in the austere Castello, the garden of the duchess (*opposite*) was arranged in the angle of one of the towers. The terrace overlooking the moats is supported by heavy machicolation and has oval apertures, which enabled the sovereigns of Ferrara to observe the city's activity. A sixteenth-century loggia with four arcades opens on to the garden, whose cool shadows are a welcome relief from the summer heat of Ferrara.

The taste for antiquity, which was so strong at the cultured court of Ferrara, is strikingly evident in the two rooms known as "game rooms" commissioned by Duke Ercole II about 1550-1555 from Camillo Filippi and his sons Cesare and Sebastiano. In the first room (*below and right*), the vault is divided into sections depicting nude athletes engaged in all sorts of games and sports. Here we see jugglers, weight throwers (the weights being heavy stone cylinders) and wrestlers. Michelangelo's influence is apparent in the powerfully muscled masculine anatomy represented in the heat of action, for Sebastiano Filippi had worked for a time at Rome under the master's direction. In the neighboring room, which is smaller (*following double page*), we again find the themes in the frieze decorated with light architectural motifs inspired by ancient "grotesques." Portrayed in the center of the vault are four dancing girls framed on either side by delightful scenes in which "putti" are playing at ninepins and spinning a top.

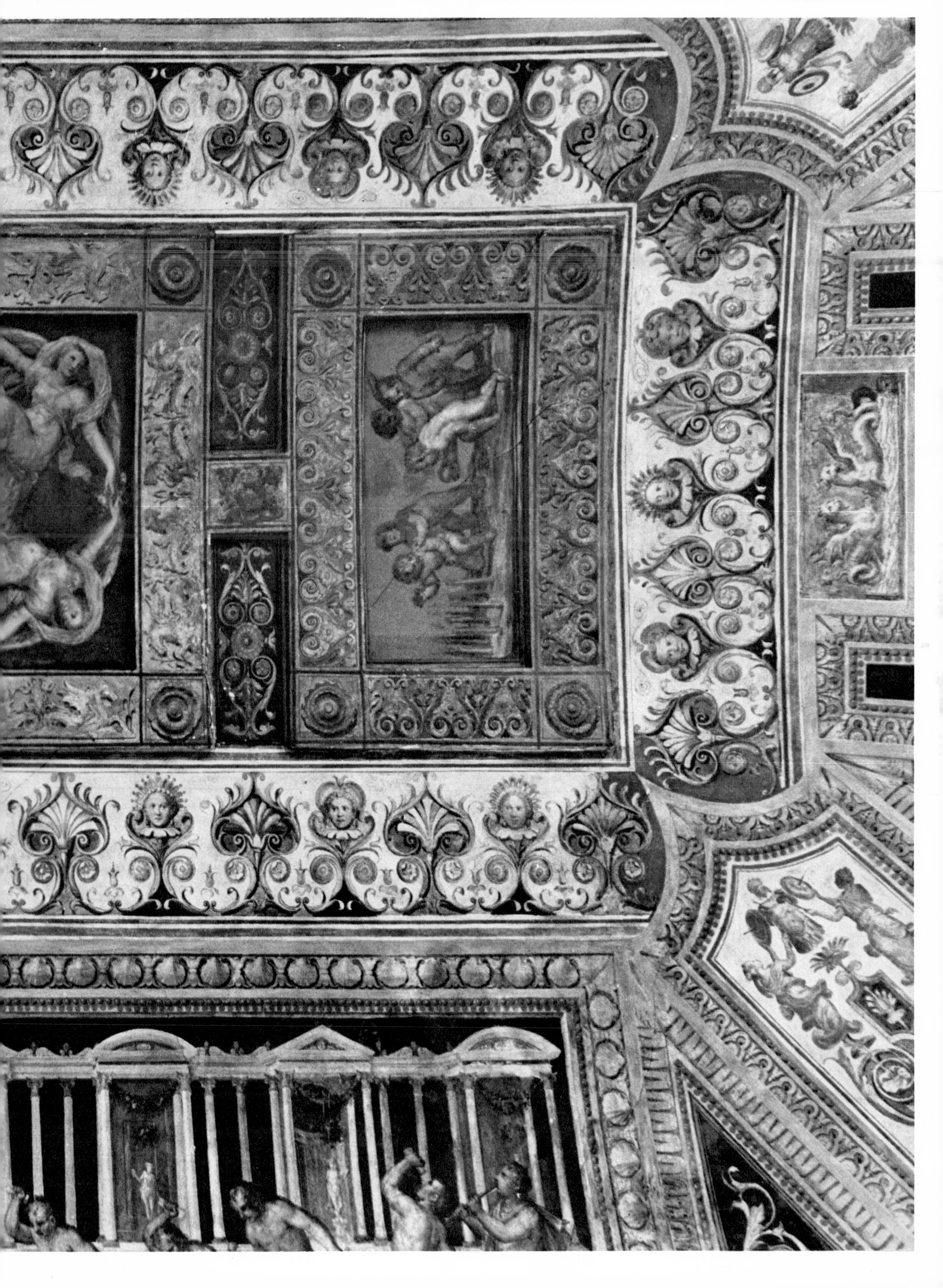

# *Rocca di Soragna*

The garden (*above*), designed in the Italian style in the seventeenth century, was completely remodeled in the English style in the early nineteenth century under the direction of the Cremonese architect Luigi Voghena. It was during this period that the artificial lake was created, the neoclassic "factory" erected and the trees and the weeping willow planted, making the park one of the most delightful examples of the "troubadour style" in Italy.

A screen of foliage veils the entrance portal opening on to the "cortile" or inner courtyard closed by four main buildings which form the castle (*opposite left*). An ancient medieval fortress, the Rocca was remodeled in the seventeenth century, losing the characteristics of a stronghold and acquiring its present more appealing mien. Numerous windows facing the courtyard partly covered by Virginia creeper ensure sufficient light for the apartments. The statues of Diana, Apollo, and Ceres with Persephone which adorn the angles date from the remodeling.

Sisera the Canaanite, commander of Jabin's army, having been defeated by Barak, commander of the Hebrews, fled and sought refuge with Jael, the wife of Haber the Kenite. Jael agreed to hide him and offered him milk; but no sooner had he fallen asleep than she took a nail and with a hammer pierced Sisera's temple. This is the episode from the Book of Judges which is depicted on one of the walls in the Room of the Stout Women (*left*), while on the opposite wall (not shown here), Judith and Holofernes are represented. The biblical heroine ferociously brandishes her hammer above the unfortunate commander, in a setting of *trompe-l'œil* architecture to emphasize the theatrical aspect of the scene, witnessed by an unperturbed, graceful feminine figure who leans over the *trompe-l'œil* balcony painted on the vault. The work of an unknown artist, the decoration dates from the close of the seventeenth century as does the superb wood-gilt console adorned with a coat-of-arms representing a wolf, emblem of the Meli Lupi di Soragna family.

In the Stucco Room (*above*), trophies, cherubs, medallions, draperies modelled in stucco with an utterly Baroque brio and decorative sense, frame cartouches revealing landscapes, seascapes, flowers and mythological figures (in the center we recognize Bacchus and Ariadne). This lavish decoration is dedicated to the glory of the Meli Lupi di Soragna family, whose triumph is painted on the ceiling. It is the work of Ferdinando and Francesco Galli da Bibbiena, assisted by Facchini, for the landscapes and seascapes, and Giovanni Bola; it was executed during the very last years of the seventeenth century.

The state apartments have preserved completely intact their decoration and the furniture which was arranged at the close of the seventeenth and beginning of the eighteenth century. In one chamber (*right*) the alcove is fronted by a triumphal arch and a carved grille which is entirely covered in gilt, one of the most extraordinary Baroque decorations in all Italy. The bed of embroidered silk and the mural tapestries of brocade and Genoese velvet are original. In the small salon (*above*) the cartouches, the cupids, the volutes and palms, executed by Giuseppe Bovi in 1701, entirely cover the walls and ceiling, forming a colorful background for the mirrors and the portraits of Giampaolo, the first Prince Meli Lupi di Soragna, and of his wife Ottavia Rossi di San Secondo. The gilt motifs, carved in very high relief, emerge from a dark background which emphasizes the striking decoration. Although the floor of the bedroom is laid in plain red slabs, that of the small salon is of marble mosaic. Here again we see the wolf and the imperial eagle which, along with figures of children, also adorn the low grille separating the alcove chamber.

# *Campania and Sicily*

*Under the yoke of seven foreign dynasties since the twelfth century, Naples was the capital of a kingdom which lasted until 1860. The famous bay dominated by Vesuvius and washed by a strong blue sea creates an enchanting setting celebrated by poets since antiquity. Palm and orange trees make the surroundings of Palermo equally pleasant, but its beauty moves us less. Sicily, wrested from the Saracens by the Normans and later held by the Hohenstaufen, was annexed to the Kingdom of Naples when the House of Aragon won it from the descendants of Charles of Anjou, brother of Saint Louis. After Charles V it was the Spanish Hapsburgs who ruled Palermo and Naples. In 1713 they were succeeded by their Austrian cousins, who reigned only a few years. In 1738 the Spanish Bourbons were given the Kingdom of Naples, but the revolutionary upheaval at the close of the eighteenth century twice forced them to seek refuge in Sicily; they were replaced by the Republic in 1799, by Joseph Bonaparte in 1806, and by Murat from 1808 to 1815. In 1860 Garibaldi seized the Kingdom of the Two Sicilies and handed it over to Victor Emmanuel II.*

## Caserta *Royal Palace*

Caserta calls for comparison with Versailles. In fact, the palace of Caserta was originally planned not as a mere château but as the center of a veritable capital, grouping ministries, a court of justice, universities "for the liberal arts, the intellectual sciences and physics," a public library, a theater, a seminary and a cathedral. Thus the project was even greater than that of Versailles. It is worth remembering that the founder of the palace, Charles VII of Naples, the future Charles III of Spain (1716-1788) was the great grandson of Louis XIV whose forceful personality exerted a strong influence beyond the borders of France, particularly on the Bourbons of Italy and Spain.

When, as a result of the intrigues of his mother Elizabeth Farnese and according to the "Family Pact," Charles VII exchanged the Duchy of Parma for the Kingdom of the Two Sicilies, "the finest crown of Italy," he found upon his arrival in Naples in 1734 merely a delapidated palace almost devoid of furniture. Indeed, the servants had the greatest difficulty in finding the necessary number of beds for the sovereign and his court. The work of refurnishing the palace, however, was rapidly carried out, for in November, 1739, Charles de Brosses considered the palace "a handsome edifice on the exterior and responding adequately to the interior." He particularly appreciated "the splendid painting of the Farnese family which had been transported here, but," he added, "these Spanish Barbarians whom I regard as modern Goths, not satisfied with having torn them while removing them from the palace at Palermo, left them for three years on a blind staircase where everyone went to urinate. Yes, Monsieur, one urinated against Guido Reni and Correggio. . . . Think of my sorrow on hearing such a baneful story!"

The king, an avid hunter, next turned his attention to erecting the pavilions enclosed by parks where he could satisfy his passion for the chase. The result was the series of villas of Procida, Capodimonte, Portici and Resina. It was not until about 1750 that he conceived of a more important royal residence, less exposed than the one at Naples to the eruptions of Vesuvius and to bombardment by the English fleet. The domain of Caserta belonged to Francesco Caetani, Count of Caserta, who some thirty years previously had been sentenced in absentia for having plotted against the Spanish viceroy. As early as 1735 Charles VII had taken advantage of this to confiscate the domain which he used as a hunting ground (the Count of Caserta subsequently received the sum of almost 500,000 ducats as compensation) and where he decided to build his new palace. He commissioned Luigi Vanvitelli to design the Palace and permission was granted by Pope Benedict XIV. On January 20, 1752, the king's thirty-sixth birthday, the first stone was laid in the presence of the queen, Maria Amelia of Saxony, the Nuncio, various ambassadors and the entire court. The stone was embedded in a foundation of gold and silver medals bearing the inscription *"Deliciae Regis, Felicitas Populi"* (the king's delight, the people's joy), a rather strange boast when we consider that the enormous enterprise was to weigh heavily on the state's finances and on the taxpayers. Charles VII had planned a total expenditure of five million ducats divided over a period of six years. In 1754, on showing the plans of the edifice to his minister to Sardinia, he stated: "I will need ten years to finish it, for I do not want to reduce the funds that I have allocated." Indeed the sums allotted were greatly exceeded, which is not at all surprising when we realize that the palace covers almost 54,000 square yards and contains 1,200 rooms and 36 staircases. The king insisted on an interior decoration of stunning richness and, upon showing the Minister of Piedmont various columns and colonnades, said: "These are samples of every marble discovered in the kingdom of Naples and in Sicily and among these the handsomest is destined to decorate the royal chapel now being built. Only the Veronese yellow is missing, but in the excavation work being carried out, there have been discovered by chance two rather large pieces. Consequently I had a part cut into very thin slabs in order to have a sufficient quantity to finish the chapel mosaics. The rest will be used for the columns and ornaments of my palace, whose vestibule will consist of thirty-two columns from a single piece."

Queen Caroline Murat and Her Children
*by Gerard*

Charles VII was never to live to see his work finished. When he stayed at Caserta in January, February and March of each year he resided at the ancient villa of the counts of Caserta. In 1759, after his departure from Naples and his ascension to the Spanish throne on the death of his half-brother Ferdinand VI, work was continued more slowly and with many interruptions. The exterior architecture was finished in 1774. Work on the park and its fountains, begun in 1762, was to last until 1780. The decoration of the apartments, though never entirely finished as planned, spanned an even longer period.

In 1768 Caserta was the scene of the marriage of Ferdinand IV, second son of Charles VII, who had succeeded to the throne of Naples, at the age of eight in 1759, and Maria Caroline of Hapsburg Lorraine, daughter of the Empress Maria Theresa and sister of Marie-Antoinette. The young couple spent the night in an apartment which had to be furnished and made ready for them at the last minute and Giovanni Paisiello's opera *l'Idolo Cinese* was performed on the stage of a makeshift theater. In the following year the present theater was finished and thereafter the court spent the first months of the year at Caserta, indulging in a series of carnival festivities. In 1770 as many as four masked balls were given during the month of February. The sovereigns then had their apartments in the south wing, on the right of the entrance portal. Like her sister at the Petit Trianon, Maria Caroline had an English garden laid out in the park (1782). Goethe, who visited Caserta in 1787, judged the palace "truly royal but with little animation. As for us, we were not at ease in these huge empty spaces."

The revolutionary period at Naples was far too turbulent to permit the luxury of new embellishments to the palace. After the rise of Napoleon, Joseph Bonaparte was named King of Naples in 1806, but he gave up the throne to his brother-in-law Murat in 1808 when he became ruler of Spain.

Murat and his wife Caroline, Napoleon's sister, often stayed at Caserta surrounded by a brilliant court. The king and queen each had a numerous "household" which was shrewdly and prudently made up of both French and Neapolitan members. Murat's Grand Chamberlain was general Colonna, Prince of Stigliano, his Master of the Horse was General Exelmans, his Master of the Royal Hunt the Duke di Cassano Serra, his Master of Ceremonies the Duke of San Teodoro Caracciolo. Among the queen's ladies of the palace were Baroness Exelmans, Mme. d'Arlincourt and Mme. Piétiet-Colbert, but her lady-in-waiting was Donna Giulia Carafa di Cassano-Serra and her lady of the wardrobe Duchess di Gallo. The choir master was Paisiello, who had served the Bourbons.

The sovereigns furnished the "appartamento nuovo" for the most part with furniture brought from France. On his return to Naples in 1815, Ferdinand IV, dazzled, is said to have exclaimed : "Papa mio! Why didn't our exile last ten years longer!" He limited himself to replacing Murat's initials with the lilies of the Bourbons and laid out a royal apartment which was finished in 1822. His successor, Francis I, commissioned the decoration of the throne room. This was interrupted by his death in 1830, but was resumed in 1839 and finished in 1845, fifteen years before the fall of the kingdom of Naples, when Caserta was acquired by the House of Savoy.

During World War II the palace was used as Allied General Headquarters in the Mediterranean. The surrender of the German army in Italy was signed here on April 29, 1945. The palace now belongs to the Italian State. The royal apartments have been converted into a museum.

## Palermo *Palazzo Gangi*

In a letter to Prince Gangi written in early February 1882, Richard Wagner wrote: "I cannot leave Sicily without thanking you and assuring you of my precious remembrance of your kindness and of the Palazzo Gangi; your devoted R.W." Indeed, Wagner had spent the winter of 1881-1882 in Sicily where he finished *Parsifal*, first at the Albergo dei Palmieri at Palermo, then in a country residence situated on the outskirts of the city which had been put at his disposal by Prince Gangi. The present Prince Gangi also kept until World War II, when it was destroyed by an air raid, a copy of the Italian score of *Lohengrin* with the dedication: "The first lines written under the hospitable roof of Prince Gangi dedicate to him the Italian transcription of the work of his very devoted and very grateful friend and servant, Richard Wagner —February 2, 1882."

The palace was erected in the first third of the eighteenth century from the design by the great Sicilian architect, Filippo Juvara, who was also responsible for the façade and staircase of the Palazzo Madama at Turin and for the royal palace at Madrid. The palace then contained a private theater which was long popular with Palermitan society. The ruin of its owners, however, was to prove almost fatal, for early in the nineteenth century it was divided into small dwellings and began to fall into disrepair. In 1820 it was fortunately acquired by Giovanna Valguarnera, Princess Gangi, who offered it as dowry to her husband, Don Giuseppe Mantenga, ancestor of the present owners.

Great art collectors, Prince and Princess Gangi restored the edifice and it again acquired its past splendor. Passionately fond of music, they received many musicians and composers at the palace, including Vicenzo Bellini, who played selections from *Norma* on a spinet. The prince and princess accumulated in their salons precious art objects, Oriental and European porcelain, furniture and rare paintings. During the period between the two world wars, George V of England and Queen Mary, Alfonso XIII of Spain, Umberto of Italy and Queen Maria-José were often received at the Palazzo Gangi. More recently the grand salon was used for the ballroom scene in Luchino Visconti's film *The Leopard* from the novel by Lampedusa.

The present Prince Gangi and his sister Princess di San Vincenzo Gangi now lovingly preserve their beautiful residence.

## Palermo *La Favorita*

On June 25, 1799, Maria Caroline of Naples wrote from Palermo to Lady Hamilton: "Finally, my dear Milady, ask Milord Nelson to treat Naples as if it were a rebellious Irish city that behaved this way; one ought not to consider the number: a thousand less villains would make France weaker and we would be all the better. They deserve to be deported to Africa or the Crimea; to deport them to France would be an act of charity. . . . Therefore, my dear Milady, I strongly advise the greatest firmness, force, vigor and rigor: the faithful populace wish it. I would like you also to give me news of you more often; you can imagine my eagerness. Believe me for life your more than sensitive, affectionate and grateful friend, Caroline."

During this period, thanks to Cardinal Ruffo's armed bands and Nelson's fleet, Ferdinand IV had regained from the French his Neapolitan estates. The queen, Marie-Antoinette's sister, thus entrusted the former courtesan, now the wife of the English ambassador Sir William Hamilton and all-powerful mistress of the English admiral, with the task of exacting vengeance against those who had adhered to the short-lived Parthenopean Republic of General Championnet. Lady Hamilton and Nelson did not fail to satisfy the queen's sanguinary taste, for the Neapolitan intelligentsia, including an important part of the liberal aristocracy, were pitilessly slaughtered, Admiral Caracciolo was hanged from the top of the mast of the *Minerva* and the Marquise da San Felice, pregnant at the time of her sentence, was executed shortly after giving birth despite the intervention of the hereditary princess, the sister-in-law of Ferdinand and Maria Caroline.

Several months earlier, deathly frightened by the approach of the French troops, the king and queen had decided to leave Naples for Sicily. On December 21, 1798, together with the royal children, including Maria Amelia, the future French queen, and their suite, they boarded the *Vanguard* in the company of Nelson, Sir William and Lady Hamilton. Before sailing away, Ferdinand carefully loaded the English vessels with the finest works of art from the palace, as well as the silver plate and crown jewels, valued at eighty-five million francs of the period. In addition, he also transported sixty-two million francs which had been removed from the state banks, leaving the Neapolitans in financial ruin.

The crossing was so bad that Sir William Hamilton held a pistol in each hand, ready to commit suicide in case of shipwreck. The young prince Albert died on December 25 when the vessel was off Palermo. The queen, prostrate with grief, disembarked at dawn the following day in order not to be recognized. The king, on the contrary, waited until the whole populace had gathered on the quay to acclaim him. The loss of his kingdom and the death of his son did not prevent him during the days that followed from visiting the sights of Palermo or holding festivities in honor of the Sicilian nobility and attending the theater. On January 7, 1799, he purchased the villa belonging to Benedetto Lombardo, Baron della Scala. Ferdinand not only wanted a country residence with huge hunting grounds, but one that provided greater comfort than the royal palace at Palermo. The edifice, named La Favorita by the king himself, was completely transformed and partly rebuilt to give it a rather Chinese aspect. The interior was luxuriously decorated either in

*Lord Nelson*

the Chinese style or in the Pompeian mode with a few attempts to give it a Turkish flavor.

Work was far from finished when, on May 17, 1799, the royal family entertained Nelson at an elaborate banquet, after which he left for Martimo in pursuit of the French fleet. On September 3 a great fête was held to celebrate the reconquest of Naples; according to some authors this took place at La Favorita, although others maintain that it was held in the royal palace at Palermo. A Temple of Fame had been erected in the gardens in which a wax statue of Victory, representing Lady Hamilton, crowned a statue of the admiral. During the fête, the king himself took the crown of diamonds from the statue and placed it on Nelson's head. After embracing the English hero he likewise crowned Lady Hamilton, and even Sir William, the cuckolded husband, whose complaisance under the circumstances must have been remarkable to see.

On the following October 4 another festivity was held—this time definitely at La Favorita—to celebrate both the birthday of the heir to the throne and to honor Nelson again before his departure. A description of the event relates that the illuminations and fireworks were "Chinese" in order to harmonize with the architecture of the villa. This leads one to think that, at least on the exterior, La Favorita was very much as we know it today.

In 1806, after a short peaceful interlude, during which they attempted to restore the court at Naples, Ferdinand and Maria Caroline were once again forced to set sail for Palermo when, the day after Austerlitz, Napoleon made Joseph Bonaparte King of Naples. La Favorita was then plunged into gloom. Although indebted to the English for preserving Sicily, the queen developed a hatred of them equal to that previously aroused by the French. Tired of her constant intrigue, Lord Bentinck, the English representative, insisted that Ferdinand send her to a quiet retreat and at the same time grant a constitution to his subjects. The old sovereign was obstinate, but in the face of English pressure, there was no choice except to grant his son, the future "King Bomba," the vicariate or regency of the kingdom. However, Ferdinand did not consider himself beaten. On February 6, 1813, he established himself at La Favorita and from there, on the 9th, went into the city where he annuled the decree making the hereditary prince regent. When he was threatened by the English, however, he suddenly made an about-face and, after a terrible fit of rage, gave his son full power and took an oath never again to mix in politics. He even went so far as to declare that he had "acted foolishly" in obedience to his wife.

Lady Hamilton *by Romney*

On the night of March 18 he returned secretly to La Favorita, forbidding entrance to anyone except close friends. Fearing another impulsive act, Lord Bentinck ordered his English troops to surround the villa to prevent the king from joining the exiled queen at Castelvetrano. Ferdinand had to yield and Maria Caroline was sent to Vienna, where she was warmly received by her son-in-law and nephew Francis I of Austria; she died at the Austrian capital in 1814. Her husband, who regained possession of Naples after the fall of Murat, followed her in 1825. In 1816 Ferdinand IV of Naples (and III of Sicily) took the title of Ferdinand I of the Two Sicilies, which gave rise to the epigram:

*You were both fourth and third.*
*Now you have become first.*
*If this continues, you will finish zero.*

La Favorita was no longer inhabited

except on rare occasions. On the fall of the Bourbons of the Two Sicilies, it was acquired by the Italian Crown, then by the city of Palermo, which arranged for its restoration (1903-1904).

## Bagheria *Villa Palagonia*

In 1787, Goethe wrote of the Villa Palagonia: "There is not a nook where the prince's madness is not evident in some extraordinary discovery." Indeed, the poet's description in his *Journey to Italy* is astonishing and corroborates that of many other travelers.

The villa was built about 1715 by Prince Ferdinand Francesco Palagonia and nothing originally distinguished it from other elegant dwellings then built by the Palermitan aristocracy, the fashion having been launched by Prince Butera at the close of the seventeenth century. It was Prince Palagonia's son, also named Francesco, who in 1747, after throwing out the furniture, antiques and portraits of the family which he had inherited, commissioned the incredible decorations mentioned with fascinated repulsion by his contemporaries.

On approaching the villa we discover strange statues perched on the wall surrounding the cour d'honneur including a woman with the head of a horse—this fantasy seems to have obsessed the prince and is found again elsewhere—seated at her *table de toilette*. Then come dwarfs, animals with several heads bristling with horns or composed of such strange combinations as a lion's head mounted on the neck of a goose "with the body of a lizard, the legs of a goat and the tail of a fox." There are more than six hundred of these figures, "a heap of monsters as revolting to the eye as removed from nature," according to the English traveler Brydone, who added that the local magistrates had begged the prince to get rid of them because of the dangerous impression they could have on pregnant women who passed that way—a request which the prince refused.

The apartments were even more extravagant. A bust of a woman, delightful when seen from one side, reveals from the other side a death head; another figure is that of a nurse rocking a child with the head of an old man; a clock is shaped in the form of a woman whose eyes move with each second's beat. In the prince's bedroom, we find sculptured in marble a multitude of repulsive animals, including toads, lizards, scorpions and snakes. The forty floor lamps which illuminated the salons were once composed of cups, saucers and teapots of Dresden china or Far Eastern porcelain.

But it is in the chapel and the sacristy—the prince was very religious and showed proof of exceptional piety when he whipped his penitents—that his folly reached its peak. In the sacristy is a marble bust of a charming woman "of refined coquetry" whose face and breast are being devoured by a host of insects and animals, scorpions, worms, centipedes and even moths. The chapel chandelier consisted of a crucifix attached to the vault; a chain emerging from Christ's navel was wrapped around the neck of a polychrome wooden figure depicting *Saint Francis Kneeling*, the hands and feet supporting candles.

In the words of Swinburne, the prince "resembled some poor luckless wight. His body is so frail and he appears so timid that no one would ever suspect him of having sufficient energy to invent such follies. It is said that when married he had hoped with all his might that his wife would give birth to a monster. He himself claimed not without humor to those who questioned him about the origin of the monsters which 'decorated' his residence that they all came from Egypt where the action of the sun's rays is so powerful on the mud left by the Nile that it brings forth all kinds of strange animals unknown elsewhere." Another visitor, the Count of Borch, stated, however, that despite these decorative eccentricities, "the prince had an enlightened mind, a strong sense of right, a rather extensive knowledge and an excellent heart."

Goethe related that one day in the Via Cassero at Palermo he saw the prince wearing court dress, with powdered wig, diamond buckles on his shoes and a sword at his side, accompanied by servants who requested money from passers-by for the ransom of prisoners captured by the Berbers. "He would do better to spend his money for this work than for his villa," the poet said to the innkeeper, who had informed him of the name of this odd person. "What do you expect," the innkeeper replied. "For our follies we gladly spend our own money but for our virtues we prefer to take money from others."

Indeed, by about 1770 the prince had spent more than 46,000 lire for these "follies" and had seriously depleted the family patrimony. His brothers and heirs finally managed to get him under their wing. "Deprived of the pleasure of creating devils," Swinburne informs us, "he turned to saints and spent his life following processions and frequenting churches."

On his death, the villa passed into the hands of his half-brother who was also his son-in-law, having at the age of sixty married his daughter, who was then ten years of age. The first thing the new prince did was to get rid of most of the monsters accumulated so lovingly by his predecessor. Later in the nineteenth century and during the first half of the twentieth, the villa was left in a state of abandonment. It has recently been acquired by the municipality of Bagheria which is having it completely restored.



Murat, King of Naples *by Gera*

# *Royal Palace*

In 1790 the Princess of Gonzaga wrote to her husband: "I arrived from Caserta, where I spent the whole day satisfying my curiosity. This is the Versailles of the Kings of Naples; the palace is a worthy residence of the masters of the world. By the grandeur of his conception and the nobility of his style, the architect Vanvitelli was the rival of Michelangelo."

The huge façade *(above)*, 759 feet long, is enlivened by a central pavilion surmounted by a pediment and two terminal pavilions adorned with columns. The edifice, begun in 1752 from the design by Luigi Vanvitelli, was finished in 1774. The architect's original design, however, was not carried out entirely, for he meant the palace to be flanked by angle towers and crowned by a central cupola, which would have balanced the composition. The park *(opposite and following pages)*, whose perspective extends for almost two miles and which covers 247 acres, was begun in 1762 but was not finished until 1780 under the direction of Carlo Vanvitelli after his father's death in 1773. Dotted by a whole series of statues and vases, the axis of the park follows an impressive succession of cascades, basins and fountains fed by a twenty-five mile aqueduct.

In the freshness of its bubbling and sparkling water, the cascade which closes the perspective of the park terminates in a basin with two groups representing the story of Diana and Actaeon who, having surprised the goddess bathing, was changed by her into a stag and torn to pieces by his own hounds. Like every statue in the vast park, these groups are the work of Neapolitan sculptors who have given free rein to their Baroque verve. That of Diana is by Angiolo Brunelli and Paolo Persico, that of Actaeon by the same Brunelli and Pietro Solari.

The grand vestibule on the first floor *(right)*, in the center of the main buildings, is in the form of a cross, breaking up the space within the palace into four inner courts. Similar in design to churches with a central plan, this vestibule consists of a rotunda opening by means of a series of eight arcades on to a circular gallery. With an extraordinary spatial grasp Vanvitelli combined the central cupolas with smaller, lateral ones and half cupolas over the apses where the doors leading to the apartments are found. The vestibule is reached by means of a majestic double flight of steps *(above)* faced with marble; the monolithic columns of the vestibule are also of marble. In a niche, beneath the vault of the ground floor, is a copy of the *Farnese Hercules*, once the pride of the Palazzo Farnese in Rome and now in the Naples Museum.

On the walls of the salon, draped in classical tunics, are the figures of Mars, Fame and Victory contemplated by Force and Prudence *(above)*. The entire decoration, executed in stucco imitating a variety of colored marble, is the work of the architect Antonio da Simone, who was assisted by the sculptors Valerio Villareale and Domenico Masucci. Begun by Joseph Bonaparte in 1807, then continued by Murat, the decoration was not finished until after the throne was restored to Ferdinand IV.

On the walls of the bathroom *(right)* of Maria Caroline of Naples, between mirrored pilasters, Rococo garlands and arabesques frame mythological subjects painted by Fedele Fischetti. Above the bathtub are *The Three Graces*. Stranger still, at the far end, is *Diana Changing Actaeon into a Stag* after he had surprised her while bathing, for modesty was certainly not the queen's chief virtue. The decoration, which was executed about 1780 in gilt stucco against a light pink and turquoise background, is still in the Rococo style although certain elements announce a return to classicism, such as the bathtub in the shape of a sarcophagus and the painted figures similar to those by Angelica Kauffmann who enjoyed great success in Naples at the close of the eighteenth century.

Palermo

# *Palazzo Gangi*

Erected in the first third of the eighteenth century from the design by Filippo Juvara, the palace consists of a most majestic entrance façade *(above)*, adorned in the center with a Baroque portal, flanked by columns supporting vases, which leads to an inner courtyard. The bulging wrought-iron balconies are typically Sicilian. The pilasters, the cornice and the window frames are painted in a stately gray which emphasizes the design against the ochre background of the walls. The windows, with their pediments either pointed or bulging, appear to have been modified at the close of the eighteenth century in the neo-classic style.

"Versailles itself can offer nothing more magnificent," wrote French author and travel writer Louis Bertrand, dazzled by the palace ballroom *(opposite)*. Indeed, the striking effect of gold colors and the glitter of the chandeliers, reflected in the mirrors tarnished by time, form a truly

enchanting setting. On the walls the paneling and mirror frames, in a frenzied Rococo motif, are entirely gilded and painted with bouquets and garlands of flowers. Consoles present a collection of Japanese and Chinese porcelain and form an integral part of the room's decoration, as was the style in the seventeenth and eighteenth centuries. The ceiling consists of a first vault of *trompe-l'œil* architectural designs opening on to a second vault where in another *trompe-l'œil* setting we see *Ceres Accompanied by Cupids,* the work of the Palermitan artist Giuseppe Velasquez. The polychrome ceramic floor represents *The Labours of Hercules.* The Venetian chandeliers date from the eighteenth century. The sofas and stools are upholstered with Aubusson tapestry commissioned specially for the occasion in the mid-nineteenth century.

# *La Favorita*

Palermo

With its "Gothic" blind arcades, its minarets, its cornices in a "pagoda" fashion, La Favorita *(above and left)* only vaguely merits its name as "palazzina cinese" or Chinese Villa as it was sometimes called. Actually it was a response to that vogue for exoticism that characterized the eighteenth century and foreshadowed the Romantic revivals.

Erected during the closing years of the eighteenth century and the beginning of the nineteenth, probably from the design by the Palermitan architect Giuseppe Patricola, the edifice is relatively small in size, at least for a royal residence. Framed by terraces and crowned by a belvedere, it consists on the ground floor merely of a large reception room, on the first of the royal apartment, followed on the second by that of the queen. Frightened by intrigues, Maria Caroline wanted La Favorita to be out of reach of foreign ears, and the service rooms, the kitchens and the servants' quarters were all relegated to the pavilion connected with the "palazzina" by an underground passage. The color of the walls, now faded, was originally of many brilliant hues. Dragons adorn the window pediments, while friezes encircle the entire villa, decorated with figures which innocently pretend to be Chinese. The balconies and cornices were originally equipped with small bells which tinkled in the slightest breeze.

Evoking the pleasures of the seraglio which Maria Caroline, although more than fifty years of age during exile at Palermo, was far from renouncing, the Turkish Salon *(above)* is covered with a delightful, finely incised decoration. The white ornamentation heightened by gold stands out against the background of various colors—dark-green false marble for the columns and pilasters, ochre and turquoise for the walls. The pointed ornamental arcades are not at all related to Moslem art but rather to that of Gothic Troubadour. But the presence of a few crescents, like that of the alabaster lamp inspired by one that may have been seen in a mosque, obviously helped to confirm the queen's self-styled role as sultana.

The King's Chamber *(right)* is treated in a Chinese style as approximate as the Turkish style of the Queen's Salon. The room is divided into three sections by rows of columns, the central one forming the alcove with its bed surmounted by a draped canopy. The walls are covered with painted cotton fabric, parts of which are now in poor condition, inspired by Far Eastern wallpaper. On the ceiling are delightful small figures leaning over a balcony in a landscape of kiosks and footbridges shaded by conifers.

# *Villa Palagonia*

"A sanctuary of foolishness," in the words of Goethe, the villa owes its fame to the extravagant statues placed here by Prince Ferdinand Francesco Palagonia from 1747 to 1770. A good number of these have since disappeared, but the statue of a young woman *(above)*, flanked by an old man and a monster, gives some idea of the prince's strange taste. Again in the words of Goethe: "One has the impression of being followed by mad creatures." Speaking of the prince, the English traveler Brydone, who visited the villa in 1770, wrote: "His madness is very curious and we are surprised that he was not locked up long ago. He has spent his entire life creating monsters and chimera infinitely more ridiculous and stranger than any imagined by a novelist."

The villa itself *(right)* was built by his father about 1715 from the designs by the architects Napoli and Daidone. The superbly Baroque entrance façade is gracefully concave and adorned with a twin flight of steps leading to the noble story.

"The prodigious number of statues surrounding the villa," wrote Brydone, "appear from the distance as a small army lined up for battle: but as one approaches and sees each figure, one feels oneself carried off to a land of illusion and enchantment." Indeed, the wall which surrounds the cour d'honneur is surmounted by grotesque figures, dwarfs, monsters, shepherds, warriors in armor, fabulous animals grouped in a fantastic universe resembling a nightmare.

Ancestral portraits adorn the grand salon executed either in white marble or marble of various colors in an attempt to imitate damask, brocade and costume trimmings. They fit into a decoration, also of various colored marble, which is characteristically Baroque. The ceiling is completely covered by mirrored plaques partly painted with *trompe-l'œil* motifs featuring birds.

The photographs are by: Brassaï 233, 235 / Boudot-Lamotte 32, 188, 196 (1 and 3), 290, 299 / Desjardins 41, 42 (1), 132, 133, 134, 135, 137, 138, 139, 140, 141, 186, 187, 189, 190, 191, 192, 197, 208, 209, 210, 211, 212, 214-215, 216, 217, 232, 233, 246, 247, 248, 249, 250 (2) / Epoca, Paul M. Pietzsch 302 / Millet 227 / Moncalvo 25, 27 / Nahmias 28, 29, 30, 31, 34, 35, 36, 37, 44, 120, 121, 122, 123, 125, 126-127, 128, 129, 130, 131, 148, 149, 150, 151, 218, 219, 220, 221, 223, 224, 225, 226, 228, 229, 236, 238-239, 240, 241, 244, 245, 286, 288-289, 291, 292, 293, 294, 295, 296, 297, 298, 300, 301, 303, 304, 305, 306 / Italian Office of Tourism 175 / Fabrizio Parisio 287 / Fulvio Roiter 78, 79, 80-81, 83, 92, 94-95, 96, 97 (2), 99, 100, 101, 260-261, 262, 263, 264, 265, 266, 267, 268, 269, 270-271 / A. Rubin-R. César 24, 26, 60, 61, 62, 63, 64, 65, 66, 67, 68, 69, 70, 71, 72, 73, 76, 77, 84, 85, 86, 87, 88-89, 90, 91, 102, 103 (1 and 2), 104, 105, 108 (2), 109, 142, 143, 144, 145, 146, 147, 152, 153, 164, 165, 166, 167, 168, 169, 170, 171, 172, 173, 178, 179, 180, 181, 182, 183, 188, 272, 273, 274, 275, 276, 277 / Albert Skira Art Editions 82 / Edwin Smith 33, 38-39, 40, 42 (2), 43, 45 (1), 46-47, 48, 49, 93, 106, 107, 184, 194, 195, 196 (2), 231, 237, 242, 243, 250 (1), 251, 252, 253, 284, 285 / Thames and Hudson, Giorgina Masson 74-75 / Ziolo 213.